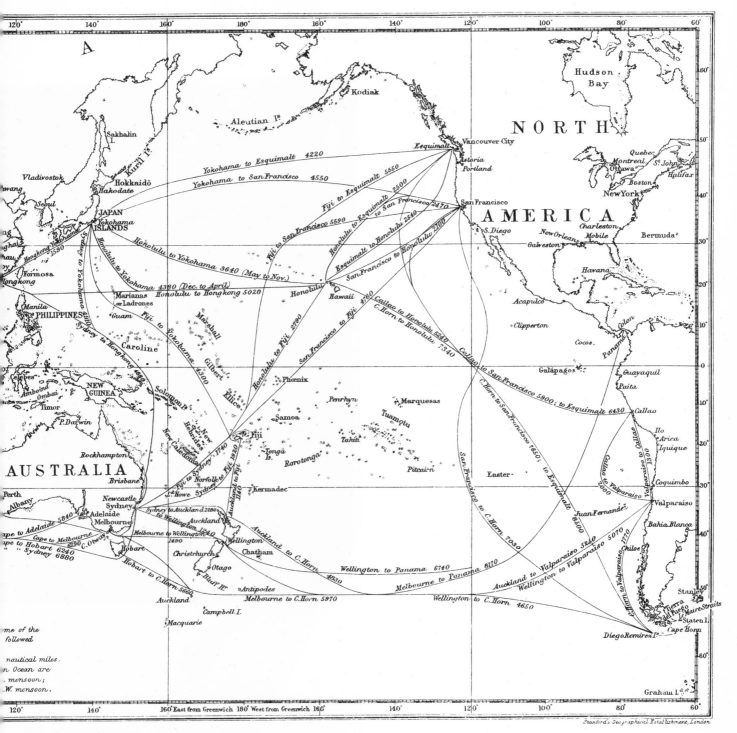

OF THE CLIPPER SHIPS

of the Controller of H.M. Stationery Office.

RUNNING HER EASTING DOWN

"Cutty Sark Running Her Easting Down" from the painting by John Spurling.

RUNNING HER EASTING DOWN

*A documentary of the development and history
of the British tea clippers culminating with
the building of the Cutty Sark.*

by

WILLIAM F. BAKER

THE CAXTON PRINTERS, LTD.
CALDWELL, IDAHO
1974

Bibliography: p.
1. Cutty Sark (Clipper-ship) 2. Tea trade—Great
Britain—History. 3. Chipper-ships—History. I. Title
VM395.C8B34   387.2′2   72-97063
ISBN 0-87004-238-6

Lithographed and bound in the United States of America by
The CAXTON PRINTERS, Ltd.
Caldwell, Idaho 83605
120709

"Through howling squalls, like a banshee's screaming
She's running her easting down.
Her bow waves whipped into spray a'gleaming
Winds from the West, now around."

AUTHOR

The selections from the poetry of John Masefield are reprinted from *Salt-Water Poems and Ballads* with permission of The Macmillan Company.

"By the Old Pagoda Anchorage" by C. Fox Smith is reprinted from *Sea Songs and Ballads 1917-22* with permission of Associated Book Publishers (International) Ltd.

Excerpts from Basil Lubbock's "The China Clippers" and "The Log of the Cutty Sark" are reprinted with the permission of Brown, Son and Ferguson Ltd., Glasgow.

CONTENTS

ACKNOWLEDGMENTS

Writing, to me at least, is, at its best, a tedious, laborious, and oft times terribly frustrating labor of love. It was the people around me, their interest, encouragement, and wonderful cooperation that made this little treatise possible. Amongst them were Mr. George Finley, who was of great help to me in locating the Spurling paintings used in the book; Mr. Ken Lawrence, editor of the Mobil Sales & Supply Corporation's publication, *The Compass*; Colonel James McGivern Humphrey, Mr. Peter Howe, Mr. Rex Vivian, and Mr. Warren Moore, for permission to reproduce their Spurlings, respectively "Thermopylae," "Cutty Sark," "Salamis," and "Blackadder;" Mr. Mark Sexton, of the Peabody Museum, who really extended himself in supplying so many of the fine photographs used in this book; the librarians at the Peabody Museum for their tremendous cooperation and seemingly infinite patience; Mr. Frank G. G. Carr, Chairman of the Ship Management Committee, the Cutty Sark Society, for permission to not only reproduce some of his fine writings, but also for the photographic research he did for me at the National Maritime Museum; my daughter Karen, who took all the photographs of the Cutty Sark used in Chapter X; my sister, Ruth Baker Coogan, of Dorset, England, who spent almost a year researching most of the material used in this volume; Mr. Llewellyn Howland III, of Little, Brown & Company, who gave me the direction that really made this book possible; and last, but by no means least, Patricia, my wife, who literally spent hundreds of hours editing this work and correcting my incredibly bad spelling.

To all of them, I am deeply indebted.

Beverly, Massachusetts
July 20, 1972

William F. Baker

~~~~~~

I MUST DOWN TO THE SEAS AGAIN!

I must down to the seas again, to the
   lonely sea and the sky,
And all I ask is a tall ship and a star
   to steer her by,
And the wheel's kick and the wind's song
   and the white sail's shaking,
And a grey mist on the sea's face and a
   grey dawn breaking.

JOHN MASEFIELD, from *Sea Fever*

How beautiful! Masefield distilled into these few simple lines all the secret yearnings of any man who has ever suffered from "Sea fever." Think a moment: have you ever let your mind wander at the sight of a tea clipper on a Christmas calendar?

Listen, do you hear the sucking of the wash around the hull, the bow wash piling high, whipped into blurring, boiling eddies? To leeward you can see the white line of the running surf booming down the beach. The lee scuppers under. The wind is coming from outer hell, the sheets are shaking, the blocks are creaking and the cold, flashing green seas crash into each other, shattering into snow.

If you love the sea; if a tall ship is your private dream; if you have ever imagined yourself, feet firmly planted on a heaving, pitching deck, at the helm of a great tea clipper under those enormous billowing clouds of white canvas; if you have ever lost yourself in all those grand dreams, then this book is for you!

This is a story of speed; not speed as we know it today with the 747s cruising at six hundred fifty mph and Apollo streaking home from the moon at seven thousand mph, but speed wedded to beauty! Speed that iron men in wooden ships wrested from the wind. Speeds that after one hundred years have never been equaled.

Those beautiful ships, lying in a thousand nameless graves, their timbers rotting in a hundred seas, can never be forgotten. Their names were like a song: Thermopylae, Hallowe'en, Sir Lancelot, Ariel, Cutty Sark . . . ah! . . . . What fantastic sailing records they set! Thermopylae ran from London to Melbourne in sixty days. Hallowe'en in one of the great annual tea races, made the passage from Shanghai to Deal, in the English Channel, in ninety days. The Cutty Sark sailed twenty-one hundred eighty miles in six days, a world's record for a six day run never equaled by any sailing ship in recorded history, making her the fastest clipper the world has ever known. Can you imagine two hundred twenty feet of wooden ship, thirty-two thousand square feet of canvas developing three thousand horsepower and racing through the seas at seventeen knots, a million pounds of tea in her hold, bound for London Town. This was the Cutty Sark. This is her story!

ILLUSTRATIONS

RUNNING HER EASTING DOWN

I

THE DEVELOPMENT OF THE
TEA CLIPPER

The "Loch Achray" was a clipper tall
With seven-and-twenty hands in all.
Twenty to hand and reef and haul,
A skipper to sail and mates to bawl.
'Tally on to the tackle-fall,
Heave now 'n' start her, heave 'n' pawl!

JOHN MASEFIELD,
from "The yarn of the *Loch Achray*"

Tea and simple economics were the cause and effect of the development of the great China tea clippers, and strangely enough, tea and economics were to cause the demise of these same clippers.

In 1599, a group of individual merchants engaged in trade throughout Asia Minor petitioned Queen Elizabeth to charter the "Honourable East India Company." In 1600, Elizabeth approved the petition and gave these merchants a monopoly on the Indian trade for fifteen years. This in itself was valuable, but even more valuable was their exemption from export duties and permission to take out currency which was ordinarily prohibited. The corporation was empowered to make laws, to export all kinds of goods free of duty, to export foreign coin or bullion, to inflict punishment, and to levy fines. It started with a practical monopoly of all the wealth to be found by trade or discovery between Cape Horn and the Cape of Good Hope. Its charter conferred the exclusive rights of trading with the East Indies, and unauthorized intruders were liable to substantial fines or loss of their ships and cargo. The Company never owned its own ships, but for many years they were supplied by the individual directors, who in turn would sell the privilege of charter to his own captain, sometimes for as much as ten thousand pounds. With the approval of the East India Company, captains who chartered from directors, were given permission to trade privately in certain commodities and to carry for his own personal account fifty tons of trade goods on the outward passage and twenty tons homeward. It was not unusual for a captain to make as much as ten thousand pounds profit for himself on a single voyage.

Tea was only an incidental in the early days of the East India Company. It was silk, coffee, and spices that were the real money-makers.

Courtesy The Peabody Museum of Salem

"The Evolution of Tea," painted by an unknown Chinese artist, depicting the entire economic cycle of the tea trade from cultivating the bushes in the hills to the loading of the "chops" on to the lighters.

In fact, it wasn't until 1669 that any quantity of tea at all was imported into England and that consisted of only two canisters weighing one hundred forty-three pounds eight ounces. This was followed in 1670 by four pots weighing seventy-nine pounds six ounces. But, tea caught the public's imagination as a rare and mystical herb from far away Cathay and consumption in the British Isles grew at an astronomical rate:

1705 .... 800,000 lbs.
1721 .... 1,000,000 lbs.
1766 .... 6,000,000 lbs.

The merchants, however, found in the East India Company an unmanageable monster structured to replenish the royal coffers by levying staggering duties on tea imports — one hundred nineteen per cent in 1784 — and like most monopolies, their inefficiencies and general dictatorial powers resulted in exceedingly high prices. It wasn't too long until a general revolt against the high-handed methods of the company by the thirty thousand wholesale and retail tea dealers in London followed. The consumers and their representatives in Parliament were soon to act. Finally, public indignation against the East India Company reached such a climax that in 1813 Parliament ended their trade monopoly in India and in 1833 finally dissolved the Company and ended their trade stranglehold on China. The East Indies and Cathay were finally open to all, on a strictly competitive basis.

As tea consumption continued to skyrocket, after the end of the East India Company's monopoly on the tea trade, merchants began to demand more rapid transportation for each of the new season's teas. The slow and stately East Indiamen, commonly known as "Tea Waggons," were rapidly becoming obsolete. These frigate built ships, slow and ponderous, with small cargo capacities, just could not supply the tremendous demands by Britain for tea from Cathay. By the mid 1850s the English people were consuming over eighty million pounds of tea annually. British ship owners, however, were slow to respond to the demands of merchant and consumer alike but not so the Americans. Seeing the enormous profits to be made in the China trade, they began an aggressive shipbuilding program to capture the cargo traffic for themselves. First came the two-masted Baltimore clipper, a great improvement over the frigate, developed during the War of 1812, and followed in 1832 by ships such as the Ann McKim. She was built by Isaac McKim, a Baltimore merchant who conceived the idea of building,

Courtesy National Maritime Museum, London

A typical "East Indiaman," so slow it was commonly known as a "Tea Waggon."
It carried the Cathay trade goods for over two centuries.

for the China trade, a three masted full-rigged vessel along the lines
of the speedy Baltimore clipper. She was built by Kennard and Wil-
liamson and named the Ann McKim, after the owner's wife. She was
framed and planked with the best materials available and fitted with
mahogany hatches and brass fittings, including twelve brass cannons.
She was four hundred ninety-three registered tons, one hundred forty-
three feet long, and thirty-one feet wide. Although the Ann McKim
proved to be one of the finest and fastest ships in the China trade,
her cargo carrying capacity was relatively small for her length and

required crew complement. Still in all, she caused a sensation when she was first put into the tea trade, despite the complacency and skepticism of shipping circles in the early 1830s. After McKim's death in 1837, she was sold to Howland and Aspinwall, New York merchants. Merchants were finally beginning to realize that tea was a cargo that was best handled quickly and that time was money.

Then came the advent of the first true extreme* clipper in 1845, the Rainbow, built by Smith and Dimon of New York for Howland and Aspinwall, followed by the Sea Witch in 1846. Speed in transporting the tea cargo was considered vital because it was believed that a long

*Considered extreme because of its length in relation to other present day ships.

Courtesy The Peabody Museum of Salem

The Ann McKim, the prototype of the true extreme clipper, caused a sensation when first put into the tea trade: New York to Anjer in seventy-nine days in 1842 and home in the spring of the following year in ninety-six days.

passage home to England spoiled the tea's flavor and fragrance. Also, the young shoots of the tea plant were harvested four times a year: the first in April for the pekoe and hyson, the second in May, the third in June and the fourth usually in September and although typically six months lapsed before the final product was ready for shipment, each successive harvest produced a coarser and less valuable and less fragrant grade of tea. Consequently there was always great competition for the young pekoes and hysons when they were ready for market. These new teas invariably went, together with top freight rates, to the ships that had the greatest reputations for speed. The first of the new season's teas, when they arrived in London each year, sold at a premium which brought additional profits to the ship owners and a substantial bonus to the captains, and of course, the fastest tea clippers of the times would command the highest freight rates in the next annual passage. So it was that the American Clippers, primarily because of increased cargo capacity and high speed, were generally able to command twice the freight rates asked by British ships. The Oriental, one thousand three tons, built in 1849, was chartered for the 1850 passage to carry tea to London at six pounds sterling per forty cubic feet while British ships went begging for London cargo at three pounds ten shillings sterling per fifty cubic foot.

So, when British ship owners finally managed to see the economics of the clipper, mostly from the high freight rates American clippers were commanding, they slowly started a building program of their own. First came the Torrington, in 1846, a two-masted clipper type schooner developed to compete with the American clipper but different in design concept in many ways. Further refinements of the Torrington's lines produced the Stornoway in 1847, and later came the Lord of the Isles, the first tea clipper to be built of iron.

British ship builders were finally on the right track. In 1885, Lord of the Isles made a remarkable run of eighty-seven days from Shanghai to London. The Americans, however, continued building clippers at an incredible rate. Jacob Bell, Donald McKay, William H. Webb, just to name a few, were building the great American merchant fleet, with clippers coming off the ways at the rate of one a week.

Not to be outdone, the British finally began an all out ship-building program. Through trial and error, new designs and refinements, the purebred tea clipper finally evolved. The Falcon, nine hundred thirty-seven tons, came off the ways in 1859 followed in rapid succession by a great fleet of tea clippers, including just to mention a few:

The first extreme clipper, Rainbow, designed by John Willis Griffiths, attracted world wide attention in 1847 when, under the command of Captain William Hayes, she made the Canton to New York passage in the remarkable time of eighty-five days.

Fiery Cross, 695 tons 1859
Taeping, 767 tons 1863
Serica, 708 tons 1863
Ariel, 853 tons 1864
Sir Lancelot, 886 tons 1864
Thermopylae, 947 tons 1868

Courtesy The Peabody Museum of Salem

The Oriental, one thousand three tons, built in 1849, was generally able to command twice the freight rates asked by British ships because of her increased speed and cargo carrying capacity.

Donald McKay's Flying Cloud, the most famous of all American Clippers, on July 31, 1851, set a noon to noon run of three hundred seventy-four miles, averaging eighteen and one half knots, at that time the greatest day's run ever made by a sailing ship.

Every one was specifically designed to challenge the Americans for the China coast trade. It all culminated with the building of the Cutty Sark, nine hundred twenty-one tons in 1869.

But clippers were only a stop gap measure and could not stem the tide towards steamships. It was rapidly becoming obvious to many merchants and a few ship owners alike that the tremendous increase in tea production, caused by the enormous world wide demand for

the beverage, and the increased market demands for other valuable
Eastern trade goods cried out for a modern method of transportation.
Steamers with their multi-million pound cargo capacity and ability to
deliver that cargo, on time, not relying on the whims of the wind for
propulsion, answered this need.

Even so, steamships tended to be looked down upon, for no steamship could match the speed of a crack sailing ship like Ariel, or the
Lightning, which once made the Liverpool — Melbourne run in sixty-
three days. Where clippers seemed to fly over the water, steamships
plodded. They required huge quantities of fuel to cover long distances,
whereas clippers only needed favourable winds — once a clipper started
out with her cargo of tea she stopped for nothing, whereas a steamship
had to keep regularly putting into port to take on more coal.

Gradually, however, the design of steamships continued to improve,
and by the end of the 1850s they were being fitted with a "compound"
engine, which used the steam twice over and was therefore much more
economical. The steamship Brandon, for example, found that this
method meant she only needed three and a quarter pounds of coal
for every unit of horsepower per hour, which was a saving of about
twenty-five per cent. She proved so cheap to run that almost all
steamships quickly converted over to the "compound" engine system.

Still another black cloud loomed on the horizon during the late
1860s: the projected opening, in 1870, of the Suez Canal. The shortcut
route through the canal would make the steamers highly competitive,
since they were able to load considerably larger cargoes than the little
clippers, and with the capability of coaling at Singapore, Port Said,
and Gibraltar, they could make the China to London run in sixty days,
a gain of a whole month over the one hundred day clippers. And, of
course, clippers would not be able to use the Canal, because they
needed to keep to the sea routes where they could pick up the trade
winds, so they would be forced to stay with the long journey round
the Cape of Good Hope.

When the Canal opened in November of 1869, only twelve and
a half percent of the world's shipping consisted of steamers, but the
percentage doubled within ten years, and by 1890 it had almost doubled
again. Clippers, which had once been the aristocrats of the high seas,
sank lower and lower, and became the tramps. By the 1890s, they had
difficulty in getting freight business for anything except cargoes which
could be kept in the holds for long periods, such as grain, timber,
scrap iron, and wool. But, it was still generally felt by the majority

of ship owners of the 1860s that the Suez Canal was not feasible, and that even if it did succeed in opening, delays in the canal, silting over, cave-ins and the intense heat of the Red Sea, resulting in the inability of stokers to work in the inferno of the boiler room, would still result in sail being a profitable and fast shipment method. In some respects they were right. Up until the beginning of World War I, steam and sail competed fiercely for long haul freight. In fact, on many long hauls, tramp steamers were not much faster nor could they offer much cheaper freight rates than sail. However, the tremendous building program of steamers during World War I foreshadowed the doom of the least efficient form of transportation.

Surprisingly, though, some of the square riggers lasted for quite a long time, and at the start of the Second World War there were still thirteen ships using nothing but sail carrying Chilean guano, Australian wool, grain, and nitrates. They looked very impressive, and one of them, the Moshulu, carried forty-five thousand square feet of sail; but they moved at a very leisurely pace, and came nowhere near the fast passages of crack tea clippers like the Cutty Sark and Thermopylae. Still, all these possible stumbling blocks did not deter many of the old hard line merchant ship owners. Even with the advent of the steamer, many tea merchants believed iron hulls caused tea to deteriorate and preferred wooden clippers for the choicest teas. So steamship or no steamship, the Scottish ship building yards in the 1860s were a veritable beehive of activity — Thermopylae was launched; Blackadder, Caliph, Wylo, Norman Court, and the Cutty Sark were on the ways, soon to be rigged and fitted out for the outward passage.

Rigging a clipper was a finely developed art requiring considerable skill. An example of what was involved in the actual fitting out and rigging of a typical crack clipper can be seen from the Caliph's outfit, Appendix B, on her maiden voyage to China in 1869. A beautiful ship of nine hundred fourteen tons, she was a very up-to-date clipper in every way. In design she was a very extreme ship with far more dead rise than any of her contemporaries. Her chief innovation, however, was her eight horsepower engine situated aft of the midship house. Besides being useful for handling cargo, lifting the anchors, pumping the ship, and hoisting the topsails, the engine was fitted with shafts for turning two small screws, which when the occasion demanded could be lowered over each side of the ship and move her along at two and a half knots in a calm. Being at sea for periods of up to four months, most of the time thousands of miles from the nearest land fall, every clipper had to be totally self-supporting and from the ship's inventory in Appendix C, it can readily be seen that very few items were overlooked. The Caliph cleared the London docks on October 12th, 1869, with general cargo, described in Appendix D, for China.

Courtesy The Peabody Museum of Salem

Photo of Sir Lancelot and Spindrift, early British tea clippers, at the Pagoda Anchorage, Foochow.

BY THE OLD PAGODA ANCHORAGE

By the old Pagoda Anchorage they lay full fifteen strong,
And their spars were like a forest, and their names were like a song.
"Fiery Cross" and "Falcon" there
Lay with "Spindrift," doomed and fair,
And "Sir Lancelot" of a hundred famous fights with wind and wave,
"Belted Will" and "Hallowe'en"
With "Leander" there were seen,
And "Ariel" and "Titania" and "Robin Hood" the brave . . .
"Thyatira" of the lovely name and proud "Thermopylae"
By the old Pagoda Anchorage when clippers sailed the sea —
Racing home to London River —
Carry on for London River —
Crack her on for London River with her chests of China tea!

By the old Pagoda Anchorage (it's many a year ago!)
A sight it was to see them with their decks like drifted snow,
And their brasses winking bright,
And the gleaming gold and white
Of the carven kings and maidens on each slim and soaring bow,
And the high and slender spars
Humming shanties to the stars,
And the hulls whose speed and staunchness are a dead man's secret
        now, —
The ships so brave and beautiful that never more shall be,
By the old Pagoda Anchorage when clippers sailed the sea —
Racing home to London River —
Crack her on for London River —
Carry on for London River with her chests of China tea!

C. Fox Smith

II
IN QUEST OF THE "BLUE RIBAND"

"Cracking on to London river,
The lee rails laid well under
Spray's 'a' stabbing like a sliver,
Will we 'ere' win, I wonder?
Thermopylae's last bearing was due west,
Oh God, but we sure got to do our best.
Now, the sea's like a sheet of steel,
The dimity seems to hang white as starch,
Will we ever feel this ship 'a' heel,
Seem we're moving to a funeral march.
Would we could slip down a green flashing crest,
'An' finally get home for a well-deserved rest."

Author

The tea clippers practically had a monopoly on the tea trade in the three decades preceeding the 1870s, so there was still a good case for the continued building of clippers even in the face of the emerging steamship.

Sail for centuries had been doing a reasonable job delivering cargo throughout the world. Sailing ships were not too costly to build and were comparatively economical to operate, and sailing, for many, was an accepted way of life. There was an adequate supply of experienced clipper captains, an abundance of good crewmen, and trade with the East was highly profitable and ever on the increase. Although the risks were enormous, the profits to be realized from a successful voyage were equally great. The American clipper Oriental, one thousand three tons, is a good case in point. The first American ship to carry a cargo of tea from China to London after the repeal of the monopolistic navigation laws, she was built for A. A. Low and Brother, New York, by

Ariel, from a painting by John Robert Charles Spurling. Her Captain, John Keay, described her as follows: "Ariel was a perfect beauty to every nautical man who ever saw her."

Jacob Bell in 1849. She was one hundred eighty-five feet long and thirty-six feet in breadth. Her maiden trip from Hong Kong by the eastern passage consumed one hundred nine days. She returned to New York with a cargo of tea in eighty-one days. On her second voyage she equaled this mark making Hong Kong in eighty-one days. Then she was chartered by Russell and Co. to carry tea to London at six pounds sterling per ton of forty cubic feet. The Oriental delivered her sixteen hundred tons of tea in London in 1850, ninety-seven days out of Hong Kong — a feat of speed never before equaled. Her original cost was seventy thousand dollars; her freight on this one shipment alone was worth forty-eight thousand dollars. On her voyage of three hundred sixty-seven days from New York through Far Eastern seas to London she had sailed sixty-seven thousand miles, logging an average of one hundred eighty-three miles a day.

Captain Andrew Shewan, of the Black Prince and Norman Court, in his *The Great Days of Sail* most picturesquely describes the loading of tea at the Pagoda Anchorage, Foochow. In the city of Foochow, after early May, when the first crop of the new teas arrived from the highlands, the Chinese merchants invariably delayed selling to foreign buyers because, amongst themselves, they just couldn't make up their minds as to what was an acceptable price. Weeks were spent in haggling, amongst themselves and the buyers alike, until finally when the price was generally agreed upon by all parties, the tea market was opened and the rush began. Speed was the first order of importance. Forty-eight hours were required to weigh and label the tea chests. Then each hong* hurried its chops** by lighter to the Pagoda Anchorage, twelve miles below Foochow, where three or four clippers with good records were chosen as "going ships." Usually, each clipper in the running had by now already loaded on board a "ground chop," which was a sufficient number of whole and half chests of inferior tea, to cover the ballast and thus provide additional protection for the fine new teas.

After weeks of idling while waiting for the market to open, suddenly, a blowing of conch shells, rockets, cannon fire, and much general hullabaloo would announce the coming of the first tea-chops. The procedure that was followed was for the coolies on the lighters to chant in a long drawn out wail the Chinese name of the hong that owned the tea. Thus Jardine Matherson's men would cry out in an unending

---

*Merchant house
**A number of boxes of the same make and quality of tea, variable as to weight, but usually the product of one particular garden.

mournful cadence: "Ee-wo! Ee-wo!" Those of Turner and Company, "Wha-kee! Wha-kee!" The din was unnerving. Captain Shewan said:

"Who it was that replied to them and directed them to their destination, I cannot say: certainly it was not members of the clippers' companies. I believe when they were expected, Chinese rivermen were stationed in anchored boats in readiness to direct them. When day dawned, hopes and fears would be set at rest. Round each of the two or three favorite ships some half-dozen or so lighters would be gathered. The rest of the fleet were out of luck and had to exercise patience. Yet they had not long to wait. In about forty-eight hours the "Blue Peter"* would be flying from the truck of one of the more fortunaté ones and the tea-chops would transfer their attention to the ship next in turn."

The arrival each year, in London of the first clipper carrying the new season's teas was a period of great interest and excitement amongst merchant, landsman, and ship owner alike. Speeding under her enormous spread of snow-white canvas from faraway Cathay to her British home port, she was "screwed tight" with the choicest of the new season's teas, meaning a handsome profit for the merchants who were the consignees of the first cargos to arrive. The best captains, the finest seamen, and the swiftest vessels on the seven seas were represented in the tea fleet.

All the world loves a winner and British ship owners were no exception. Like today's "triple crown" of horse racing, the "Indy 500," the Americas Cup races, winning the "Blue Riband of the Sea," awarded to the tea clipper making the fastest passage in the great annual China Tea Race from Foochow to the English channel, was the great ambition of many a ship owner during the era of the 1850s. To own the clipper that brought home the first teas from China heaped great personal honor on the owner, national fame for the ship, and a guarantee of top freight rates for the next season's cargo. In 1856 merchants offered for the first time a prize of one pound sterling per ton on the freight for the ship that would arrive first with the new teas, and a very exciting race took place that year between the Maury, an American clipper, and the Lord of the Isles, the British clipper commanded by Captain Maxton. To show how far clipper development had progressed between American and British ship builders, it's only necessary to state that both passed Gravesend on the same morning within a few minutes of each other.

*A signal flag flown from the top of the foremast signifying a ship was making ready for sea.

Sometimes the crew of the winning ship received as much as five hundred pounds sterling, a small fortune in those days, from the owners of the cargo, since the first teas put on the market realized from three-pence to sixpence a pound more than teas arriving later on slower ships.

The racing of tea ships, during this period of history, was an all absorbing topic in business establishments, on the dock and by the fireside. The winner gained something more substantial than mere fame — not infrequently a fortune was the prize.

In tea merchant offices, telegrams announcing the time at which tea clippers passed navigational markers were read with as much eagerness and anticipation as today's stock market quote board, and when word arrived that the clippers were beating their way up the channel, the excitement became intense: the finish was at hand. C. Fox Smith, in *The Return of the Cutty Sark*, tells the story of the Thermopylae at the end of her record breaking maiden voyage, Melbourne to London in sixty days, a record never again equaled by a sailing ship, that upon picking up her pilot at Beach Head, Captain Kemball pointed to the ship's rail and said to the pilot:

Thermopylae, considered by those who sailed her to be the most beautiful and fastest of all British tea clippers. She once set a London to Melbourne record of sixty days that has never been equalled.

"Do you see that?"

"Yes," replied the pilot, not a little surprised.

"So do I," replied Captain Kemball, "for the first time since leaving China!"

In 1862 the clipper Flying Spur, built by the firm of Messrs. A. Hall and Co., won the Great China Tea Race and received one pound sterling extra per ton for her tea cargo. During 1863/64/65 there were some very close races between Serica, the Taeping, and the Fiery Cross, which won four of the Great China Tea Races during the 1860s.

But, the most incredible ocean race of all times must have been the Great Tea Race of 1866. This remarkable event started on May 29, 1866, from the Pagoda Anchorage at Foochow and ended ninety-nine days later in London. The tea was packed and ready for shipment, barges brought it down-river to the Pagoda Anchorage near Foochow where the fastest clippers in the world were waiting. Amongst them were Ariel, eight hundred fifty-three tons, Captain Keay, the favorite; Taeping, seven hundred sixty-seven tons, Captain McKinnon; Serica, seven hundred eight tons, Captain Innes; Taitsing, eight hundred fifteen tons, Captain Nutsford; and Fiery Cross, six hundred ninety-five tons, Captain Robinson. The leaders, Taeping, Ariel, and Taitsing, each carried over a million pounds of tea.

Ariel finished loading her cargo first, three hundred ninety-one chests and two hundred twenty half-chests — a total cargo of 1,230,900 pounds — but got off to a bad start and had to anchor before the tide had fallen. She was soon passed by Fiery Cross, which got to sea first and quickly piled up a day's lead. Taeping and Serica crossed the bar at Foochow together. At Anjer, on July 15th, Ariel had made up most of her first day's loss, and she rounded the Cape about an hour behind Fiery Cross; Taeping followed twelve hours later. Unknowingly, in the passage up the Atlantic, all five ships got closer and closer to one another. At St. Helena, on August 4th, the order was Taeping, Fiery Cross, Serica, Ariel, and Taitsing. In the doldrums Fiery Cross was becalmed for twenty-four hours, and this cost her the race. Ariel had better luck; having good winds, she overtook Serica at the equator.

Early on September 5th, Ariel and Taeping passed Bishop and St. Agnes lights, and all day the two ships raced up the channel together, almost abeam, going fifteen knots. With the wind well abaft the starboard beam, both were flying all the canvas they could carry, including their skysails and stunsails. At the Downs they were only ten minutes apart, in

GREAT RACE

OF THE

TEA SHIPS,

WITH THE FIRST

NEW SEASON'S TEAS.

PRICE OF TEAS REDUCED.

THE "Taeping," "Ariel," "Fiery Cross," and "Serica" have arrived, with others in close pursuit, with something like FORTY-FIVE MILLION POUNDS OF NEW TEA on board—half a year's consumption for the **United Kingdom.** This enormous weight coming suddenly into the London Docks, Shippers are compelled to submit to **MUCH LOWER PRICES,** in order to make sales.

We are thus enabled to make a Reduction of FOURPENCE in the pound.

4/0 down to - - 3/8
3/8 „ - - 3/4
3/4 „ - - 3/0

And so on downwards.

We may add the above Ships have brought a few lots of most unusual fine quality.

Reduction takes place on Friday the 21st inst.

135, OXFORD STREET;
57, STRETFORD ROAD;
171, STRETFORD ROAD—
    "Great Northern." } **BURGON & CO.,**
TEA MERCHANTS.

Poster advertising the Great Tea Race of 1866. Like most advertising, somewhat misleading; the tea cargo of the four leaders was approximately four and one half million pounds, not forty-five million as the poster states.

a race across three-quarters of the globe. The times of the five ships at Deal were as follows:

Ariel, at 8 a.m., Sept. 6 . . . . 99 days out
Taeping at 8:00 a.m., Sept. 6 . . . . 99 days out
Serica at noon, Sept. 6 . . . . 99 days out
Fiery Cross, during the night, Sept. 7 . . . . . 101 days out
Taitsing, forenoon, Sept. 9 . . . . 101 days out

However, the race wasn't finished until the sample boxes of tea were tossed ashore at the docks in London. The excitement was intense. The progress of the contending ships up the Channel was flashed up the coast. The owners of the two leaders were so afraid of losing the ten shillings extra per ton over an argument as to which ship really won, that they secretly agreed to divide the premium, to be claimed by the first ship to dock. Of course, the captains knew nothing of this and stuck it out to the gruelling finish.

At the end it was largely a battle of the tugs. Taeping got the first tug and, to avoid the possibility of Ariel getting a faster one, her captain hired the next tug also, so that it was several hours before Ariel finally got her tow. At Gravesend, Taeping was fifty-five minutes ahead. Even so, Captain Keay's ship, Ariel, reached East India Dock entrance first at nine p.m., but, because of the tide it was ten twenty-three p.m. before Ariel hove to inside the dock gates.

Meanwhile Taeping had preceded Ariel up the river, but Captain McKinnon did not reach his berth until ten p.m., as Taeping, being some distance further up the Thames, had much farther to go to reach the entrance of London Docks. "Drawing less water than 'Ariel,'" says Captain Keay in his log, "also, the dock having two gates they got her inside the outer gate, shut it, and allowed the lock to fill from the dock; then they opened the inner gate so she (Taeping) docked some twenty minutes before us."

A more unsatisfactory finish could hardly be imagined. It was poor sportsmanship to divide the stakes. Shipping men generally agreed that after such an exhibition of racing seamanship the race should have finished when the leading ship took her pilot. A member of the crew of the Ariel in this memorable race, once wrote: "On the merits of the race under sail all honour is with the 'Ariel' for we were fully five miles to windward of the 'Taeping' when the tug boat hove in sight, and, without the assistance of steam, must have won the race."

Serica reached the West India Dock at eleven-thirty p.m., just as

Lithograph of the Great Tea Race of 1866. Taeping in the forefront, Ariel to leeward beating up the English Channel. Sixteen thousand miles, ninety-nine days of ocean racing halfway around the world with only ten minutes separating the runner-up from the victor.

the gates were closing; thus, Ariel, Taeping, and Serica, after crossing the bar at Foochow together, all docked in the Thames on the same tide.

Sixteen thousand miles, ninety-nine days of racing "hell bent for election" more than halfway around the world and only ten minutes separating the runner-up from the victor. Yes, a truly fantastic feat of ocean racing!

III

IN THE TEA TRADE

Oh I'll be chewing salted bone and biting flinty bread,
And dancing with the stars to watch, upon the fo'c's'le head,
Hearkening to the bow-wash and the welter of the tread
Of a thousand tons of clipper running free.
JOHN MASEFIELD, from "A Pier-Head Chorus"

At the peak of the tea era during the late 1860s, there were more than sixty tea clippers in the China trade, and they could be broken down into three distinct groups. First came the "old workhorses," long time in the trade, but with no noted ability for speed. Secondly came the purebreds, all capable of one hundred day passages. And thirdly, the "heirs apparent to the throne," the out-and-out racers designed for speed, built by loving ship owners, to win "The Blue Riband of the Sea."

The old workhorses included Falcon, Fiery Cross, Flying Spur, Forward Ho, Belted Will, and Thyatira. Falcon, built in 1859 by Steele of Greenock, was considered to be the first clipper to be a radical departure from all previously built clippers of the early 1850s. She was designed with less sheer, much less freeboard, lower bulwarks, and somewhat less breadth, all adding to her slim graceful appearance. She was in many ways the prototype of all great clippers to come. In the 1859 tea race she won "The Blue Riband of the Sea" by making the Shanghai to London run in one hundred six days. Again, in 1860, she beat all contenders making the homeward passage in one hundred ten days.

The Fiery Cross was built in 1860, and in the trade, was always a brilliant performer, winning "The Blue Riband" in 1861, 1863, and 1865. But win or lose, until truly extreme clippers were built, she was always a serious contender, losing the 1864 and 1866 races by a margin of only twenty-four hours.

Blackadder. Built in 1869 for Captain John Willis of London. From the painting by the late J. R. C. Spurling.

The Flying Spur was built in 1860 for Jardine Matherson & Co., the great China merchants, still very much in business today and headquartered in Hong Kong. She was a very fast little ship, but lacking the "driver" so necessary to win, she was never able to show her full colors.

The Belted Will suffered very much the same fate as Flying Spur, never having had a "driver" as master. Her performance, although she was very fast, was always "less than satisfactory."

After the decline of the tea trade, the Falcon was sold to Australian shipping interests and was finally wrecked off Java in 1871. The Flying Spur suffered much the same fate, being wrecked ten years later on the rocks off Martin Vaz Islands in the South Atlantic.

Although their records in the tea trade were outstanding by the standards of the day, as shown in the following chart, they were "tea waggons" compared to the purebreds.

Courtesy The Peabody Museum of Salem

A very rare photograph taken at Foochow in 1866, showing left to right: Black Prince, Fiery Cross, Taeping, Ariel, and Flying Spur.

1862 TEA RACE

Ship	From	Date	To	Date	Days Out
Fiery Cross	Foochow	May 28	London	Sept. 27	122
Flying Spur	Foochow	June 2	London	Oct. 9	119
Falcon	Shanghai	June 13	London	Oct. 13	122

The purebreds included Taeping, Serica, Ariel, Sir Lancelot, Taitsing, Titania, Leander, Lahloo, Undine, Windhover, and Kaisow. Listed here are some of their records set during the 1869 and 1870 passage, China to London:

	1869 Days Out	1870 Days Out
Taeping	102	112
Serica	111	118
Ariel	108	—
Sir Lancelot	98	104
Taitsing	—	121
Titania	110	112
Leander	106	98
Undine	124	105
Windover	148	99
Kaisow	99	99

Taeping, the prototype and forerunner of Ariel, Sir Lancelot, and Taitsing, was an exquisite little ship of seven hundred sixty-seven net tons. With long, narrow lines and small deck houses, her rails, decks and bulwarks of India teak, under full sail she was a dazzling sight to see. She was wrecked in 1872 off Ladds Reef, bound from Amoy to New York. Serica, too, was lost, with all hands, except the bosun, on the Paracels, in the South China Sea. Thus, **Ariel**, combined with Titania, were considered to be the most perfect examples of the purebred clipper. Ariel, who beat the Taeping by ten minutes in the Great Tea Race of 1866, was one of the most beautiful clippers ever to leave the ways. Her Captain, John Keay, who commanded her most of her days, describes her in a letter to Basil Lubbock with a certain song in his heart.

Ariel was a perfect beauty to every nautical man who ever saw her: in symmetrical grace and proportion of hull, spars, sails, rigging and finish, she satisfied the eye and put all in love with her without exception. The curve of stern, figurehead and entrance, the easy sheer and graceful lines of the hull seemed grown and finished as life takes shape and beauty. The proportion and stand of her masts and yards were all perfect.

It was a pleasure to coach her. Very light airs gave her headway

The Taeping, one of the early British tea clippers, built in 1863. Photographed in China.

and I could trust her like a thing alive in all evolutions; in fact she could do anything short of speaking.

Ariel was lost at sea on her way from London to China, in 1872, with Captain Cacheivaille in command.

At the end of her days as a crack tea clipper, Sir Lancelot went into the Indian coastal trade. This superb little ship, well known up and down the Indian coast as the "yacht of the Indian Ocean," foundered in a cyclone, in the fall of 1895, near Sand Heads at the mouth of

The Pagoda Anchorage showing, center, Serica, right the Lahloo. The other ships in this photograph are unidentifiable.

the Hooghly. Taitsing left Swansea with coal for Zanzibar and was totally lost off Querimba Island, September, 1883. Titania, Ariel's competitor in the Great 1866 Tea Race, after years of service in the China trade, was finally broken up at Marseilles in March, 1910. Leander ended up in the Indian coasting trade and came to her end, during the same Bay of Bengal cyclone that claimed Sir Lancelot. Lahloo remained in the China trade and met her doom off Sandlewood Island on July 31, 1872. Windhover was wrecked off the Australian coast in 1888, and Kaisow was abandoned on her beam end sixty miles W.S.W. off Valparaiso, Chile, in November, 1890.

Amongst the newcomers, the challengers for the "The Blue Riband of the Sea" were the Caliph, Norman Court, Wylo, Duke of Abercorn, Thermopylae, Blackadder, Hallowe'en, Spindrift, and Cutty Sark. Some of their record passages are listed below for the 1869 and 1870 outward passages.

	Days Out 1869	Days Out 1870
Caliph	111	Lost at sea
Norman Court	105	105
Wylo	103	112
Duke of Abercorn	127	119
Thermopylae	—	105
Blackadder	262 Dismasted	
Spindrift	Wrecked	
Cutty Sark	104	110

Hallowe'en and Blackadder were sister ships owned by Captain John Willis, builder of the Cutty Sark, and, in fact, were considered by many to be the models after which the bow of the Cutty Sark was designed. Hallowe'en ran ashore at Sewer Mill Lands, Salcombe, on January 17, 1887, and was totally lost. The star-crossed Blackadder, after years of bad luck, was finally lost off Bahia, April 9, 1905. Wylo spent her final days in the China to New York trade, while Caliph, an extremely fast clipper, disappeared in the China Sea on her second voyage. Little Norman Court, considered to be the most yacht-like of all the tea clippers, was wrecked in Cymmeran Bay, Anglesea, Australia, on March 29, 1883. Spindrift, one of the finest and fastest of all the tea clippers, was wrecked off Dungeness, November 21, 1869. Thermopylae, considered by some, particularly those who sailed her, to be the most beautiful and fastest of all clippers, was built by Hood of Aberdeen in 1868 for George Thomp-

Courtesy The Peabody Museum of Salem

Whampoa, a painting by an unknown Chinese artist showing two tea clippers awaiting their "chop."

son & Co. She was nine hundred forty-eight registered tons, length two hundred twelve feet, breadth thirty-six feet and depth twenty feet nine inches. Like all Thompson's ships, her hull was painted green from the copper up, an unusual departure from the standard "clipper black," with white yards and lower masts. She carried a handsome figurehead of the famous Spartan warrior Leonidas and must have really been quite a sight to see. She set many sailing records, including a Newcastle N.S.W. to Shanghai run in twenty-eight days, and set a never to be beaten record of sixty-three days from London to Melbourne. At the end of her career as a wool clipper, she was sold as a training ship to the Portuguese Government and renamed Pedro Nunez. By 1907 it was obvious that she was on her last legs, but her owners felt that she deserved something better than being broken up for scrap. So she was towed out into the Bay of Cascais off Tagus, Portugal, by two warships, and sunk by naval gun fire. She was thirty-nine years old at that time.

It's sad to note the final end of those beautiful little ships.

> Her masts were gone and afore you knowed
> She filled by the head and down she goed.
> Her crew made seven and twenty dishes
> For the big jack-sharks and the little fishes,
> And over the bones the water swishes.
> JOHN MASEFIELD, from "The Yarn of the *Loch Achray*"

So it is that today only the Cutty Sark remains, enshrined forever, at Greenwich, England, a fitting monument to the great days of sail, to the tenacity of the British seaman, and as a memorial for all lovers of the sea. As the last and sole remaining vestige of perhaps the greatest sailing era the world has ever known, step aboard with me and perhaps you too will feel that very special bond that existed between these iron men and their wooden ships.

~~~~~~

IV

LORD, WHAT A HANDSOME SHIP SHE BE

> Lord, what a handsome ship she be!
> Cheer her, sonny boys, three times three!
> And the dock side loafers gave her a shout
> And the red-funneled tug-boat towed her out. . . .
>   JOHN MASEFIELD, from "The Yarn of the *Loch Achray*"

The Cutty Sark was built for Captain John Willis, retired shipmaster — who earned his spurs and made his fortune in the China trade. His burning ambition was to beat Thermopylae and the other great clippers and win the "Blue Riband" of the great annual tea race. She was designed and built by the young firm of Scott & Linton, Dumbarton, Scotland, who took the building contract at seventeen pounds sterling a ton. A very low price even in those days but building a successful tea clipper was vital to the continued growth and success of the little firm. Willis, the cantankerous, hard headed, old sea captain, drove a stiff bargain with Scott & Linton, who badly wanted the contract. The young fledgling firm had only built five ships before, and the Cutty Sark was to be the biggest and most important but unfortunately the last ship Scott & Linton was to build.

Willis apparently wrested one additional contractual condition from Scott & Linton: he could appoint his own man to supervise construction with the power to accept or reject any materials that did not meet the letter of the contract. Willis selected one of his favorite and most trusted captains, George Moodie, for the job and Moodie did not disappoint John Willis.

John Willis took a personal interest in the design and construction of his pride and joy . . . his love. It is believed that, at Willis' suggestion, the bow of the Cutty was modeled after The Tweed, one of Willis' fastest and most favored ships. The rest of the design was totally from the board of Linton, who gave her the square stern and bilges and

Captain John "White Hat" Willis, owner of the Cutty Sark.

less tumblehome than other clippers of her day. Here was the spark of genius, for the combination of The Tweed bow and Linton's stern and bilge lines produced a ship that had tremendous power in going to windward and still a very easy ship to handle in a big following sea. In copying The Tweed, the Cutty was designed with not too much rake to her forefoot and with the forefoot rounded less than the Thermopylae or Spindrift. Additionally, Linton was greatly impressed with the sailing ability of Firth of Forth fishing schooners, known for their great heavy weather sailing ability, and designed the Cutty's midsection after these fishing boats, a design much squarer than any other clipper of her day.

So, blending together the best of The Tweed, the hull lines of the Scottish fishing boats, and his square stem concept and counter design, the Cutty Sark emerged as a hull design never before built nor ever to be duplicated. In themselves, the Cutty's lines showed potential for tremendous power and an ability to cut the water. In fact, her fine knife-like bow created considerable arguments amongst builders and ship owners alike as to her ability to develop any power. They harbored the fear that she might drive into the waves since her bow was so fine. But, they were all proven to be wrong and Linton right. She could run before the heaviest of westerlies with very little helm and keep exceptionally dry aft because of her tremendous ability to "almost plane" in huge following seas. Throughout the entire tea fleet, the Cutty had the reputation for being "best on the wind and driest on the run."

She was built as a composite clipper, a construction technique consisting of building a ship with iron frames and a wooden skin, the skin being rock elm from the keel to the sheer plank and teak from there on up. Aside from being an extremely advantageous method of construction — since it combined the strength, lightness, cheapness, and the minimum space requirements of iron with the flexibility and pliability of wood and the minimum of friction resulting from copper sheathing on a wooden bottom — the composite clipper was a welcome

Courtesy National Maritime Museum

Hercules Linton, the thirty year old designer of the Cutty Sark.

The depth of the forefoot let the Cutty Sark cut through the seas like a knife.

innovation to shipbuilders who were beginning to worry over the cost and scarcity of timber but who held to the prevailing belief of the 1850s that wooden ships were superior to those of iron.

Captain Willis was a great lover of teak and none was spared on the Cutty, with three and one-half inch teak decks, teak paneled deck houses, and six inch teak hull planking, teak even to the "harness casks."

Her spar plan was much squarer than most of the tea clippers of her day, with all her main mast and fore mast yards being interchangeable. Her main and fore yards measured seventy-eight feet with her main and fore royal yards measuring thirty-eight feet. Her main mast from deck to truck measured one hundred forty-five point nine feet, half a football field, and her foremast one hundred twenty-nine point nine: under full sail she was a veritable cloud of canvas, carrying thirty-two thousand square feet. Her registered measurements were: net tonnage nine hundred eighteen, length two hundred sixteen point six feet, breadth thirty-five point two feet, and depth twenty point five feet.

The Cutty Sark's hull was painted black up to the bulwarks, which were painted white and topped with a bright brass rail all around. The figurehead melded into beautiful gold gilt scrollwork at the cheeks

An example of "composite construction:"
iron frames and wood planking.

and a gold stripe all around, level with the main deck. The stern also had elaborate hand carved gold gilt scrollwork. The ship's name and "Port of London" were hand carved in gold gilt, raised letters entwined in wreaths of laurel upon her stern, and carved upon a crest on her taffrail was the inscription "Where there's a Willis a way." Her lower masts were welded iron tubing painted white, yards and upper masts black with her doublings and mastheads white and her boats white. Deck houses were white with inlaid teak panels.

As a tea clipper she typically loaded one million three hundred thousand pounds of tea, while in the wool trade a typical cargo, listed in the 1885 manifest, was:

     4,465 bales of wool
     2,342 packages of cobalt ore
     1,345 bags of nickel ore
     29,772 horns
     122 cwt shank bones
     76 cwt hoofs
     1 cwt of pith and 6 bales of sheepskins

Cargo battens, bolted to the iron ribs, over which the dunnage was placed to protect the valuable tea cargo.

Her heaviest cargo is believed to have been one thousand two hundred ninety tons of scrap iron which she carried from London to Shanghai, and as a coal carrier she usually loaded about one thousand one hundred fifty tons.

For all the romantic and lofty names given to clippers both British and American — Lord of the Isles, Falcon, Fiery Cross, Spindrift, Flying Spur, Glory of the Seas, Winged Racer and Flying Cloud — it is difficult to imagine Captain John Willis naming his beauty, his pride and joy, "Cutty Sark." Perhaps, like all true Scotsmen, it was his love for Robert Burns' lyric poetry. Perhaps Nannie conjured up in his mind's eye some fleeting vision of speed. We'll never know for sure. But name her thus he did.

And why the quandary over the name Cutty Sark? Well, translated from Scots, a cutty sark was generally considered a scanty, shorty night-gown commonly worn by "women of the night" and made famous as the regalia worn by Nannie the witch, in Robert Burns' poem "Tam O'Shanter."

> Her cutty sark, o' paisley harn,*
> That while a lassie she had worn,
> In longitude though sorely scanty,
> It was her best, and she was vauntie.**

But the Cutty Sark carried her name with pride, and every sailor man who ever served on her spoke the name with a special tone of lofty reverence.

No story of the Cutty Sark is complete without mention of her figurehead. Like all ships of old, the figurehead was a vital part of her fitting out. In fact, oft times, as much thought went into the figurehead as to the design of the ship itself. The Cutty Sark's figurehead was no exception. It was carved by F. Hellyer of Blackwall, one of the foremost wood carvers of his day. For the "Cutty" he carved a likeness of Nannie, her black hair flying in the wind, wearing her "cutty sark," and reaching out in hot pursuit, in a futile attempt, to grasp the tail of Tam O'Shanter's mare, Meg. The head and outstretched arm of the original figurehead were lost during rough weather in the roaring 40s. There is today, on view aboard the Cutty Sark, the Long John Silver figurehead collection, the last remains of over one hundred famous

---

*harn; coarse linen
**vauntie; proud of it

merchantmen. Should you ever be fortunate enough to visit the Cutty Sark, the museum guide may tell you an amusing little story as to how a certain unmentionable part of Nannie was perfectly repaired at a cost of only a few pence.

It is believed in many circles that Captain Moodie's diligence in supervising the construction of the Cutty Sark, inspecting every board foot of timber, every fitting, every fastening, and rejecting every bit of material that wasn't completely perfect, resulted in the financial failure of Scott & Linton. The firm of Denny Brothers of Dumbarton, took over the building contract, upon the failure of Scott & Linton,

"Nannie, her black hair flying in the wind, wearing her 'cutty-sark o'paisley harn,' reaching out in hot pursuit, in a futile attempt to grasp the tail of Tam-O-Shanter's mare, Meg. Since witches can't cross water, Tam will be safe if Meg can carry him over the bridge."

The Cutty Sark

Max Millar's line drawing of the Cutty Sark, fully rigged and loaded with tea chests.

Courtesy of Dr. and Mrs. Kirkaldy-Willis

Cutty Sark as a tea clipper, painted in 1872 by F. Tugday for Captain John Willis.

and finished the ship. She slid down the ways, with no great fanfare, on November 23, 1869. She was then towed to Greenock to be masted and rigged. Finally, on a grey London morning, in February, 1870, Captain Moodie in command, the Cutty Sark slipped away from her loading berth with general cargo for China. A passage towards immortality.

The Cutty Sark proved to be a magnificent sailor, as this story will relate as we follow her through the seven seas. But, just to stimulate your imagination, let it be said here that she was reputed to be capable of coming about faster than any other clipper ever built, to be able to sail closest to the wind of all the tea clippers of that era, and of course to having a fantastic ability to "run her easting down."

One of the Cutty Sark's apprentices on her 1883 outward passage gives us a little insight into what she was really like:

    The accommodation for apprentices in the 'Cutty Sark' was in a small house situated aft of the mainmast, and eight of us lived in a space of about fifteen feet by twelve feet. We were, however, very comfortable and happy except when she was taking water aboard, when it was nine chances out of ten if we escaped a ducking as we opened or shut the door. Although the 'Cutty Sark' was a ship that would stand up to be driven she was very lively in a heavy sea, and used to jerk instead of lying down easily to an extra gust of wind. Running the Easting Down, she simply flew through the water, and, standing at the wheel, it was terrifying to see the huge seas rolling up after her. When she dipped her stern they looked as if they were going to swamp her, but I never saw her poop at sea. . . . She was magnificent to sail by the wind, for I have been at the wheel for two hours and never moved the spoke out of my hand, just the distance that my arm could go being sufficient to steer her by.

In the southern latitudes, known as the roaring 40s, and considered by most experienced sailors to be the most dangerous sailing grounds in the world, the prevailing winds are westerly and the customary route to the East was around the Cape of Good Hope into the "roaring 40s;" picking up the hard blowing prevailing westerly and "running before the wind," i.e. to Australia. This is called, in sailorman's lingo, "running her easting down." The winds in the 40s were so powerful that ships

Painting of the Cutty Sark off Hong Kong by an unknown Chinese artist.

had to be specifically designed to withstand the tremendous force of the wind which strained hull, rigging, and spars to their breaking point. In fact many ships were actually lost in attempting to "run their easting down;" not so the "Cutty." She sailed her best and made her greatest speed distance records in the roaring 40s.

The following excerpt from the Cutty Sark's log of 1885 is an excellent example of her ability to "run her easting down."

May 9 — Lat 39° 52'S, Long 75° 03'E course N.80° E Distance 336 miles. Moderate S. W. gale, hard squalls.

May 10 — Lat 40° 12'S, Long 82° 31'E course S 86° E Distance 334 miles. Strong S.W. wind, high sea.

May 11 — Lat 39° 04'S, Long 89° 05'E course N 77° Distance 314 miles. Fresh S.S.W. wind and fine.

This calculates out, correcting for current drift, to nine hundred eighty-four miles in seventy-two hours, an average of almost fourteen knots/hour; a tremendous feat for a ship loaded down to a draught of twenty-one feet and carring *2,580,000 pounds of scrap iron* to Shanghai.

V
"CRACKING ON THE DIMITY"

An' Bill can have my sea-boots, Nigger Jim can have
    my knife,
You can divvy up the dungarees an' bed,
An' the ship can have my blessing, an' the Lord can
    have my life,
An' sails an' fish my body when I'm dead.
      JOHN MASEFIELD, from "The Turn of the Tide"

Before we progress any further, let me introduce you to these "iron men" and, "by God," iron men they were. They endured endless days of soaking, drenching rain with as little disdain as we do by wetting a foot in a puddle. They labored for days on short rations, cold uncooked food with as little concern as we do when we perhaps might occasionally miss our "morning coffee." They were driven in their labors day after day with only a few hours' sleep at a time and with no more grumbles than we might offer when "occasionally" we have to break our routine and wake a half-hour early to make that "breakfast meeting."

Because of the vast distances they covered in all weather, clipper ships and their crews had to be prepared for every conceivable misfortune that man or God could devise. Struck by lightning, battered by storms, damaged in collisions, run aground, becalmed, half-starved, dismasted in cyclones, set on fire, and ravaged by scurvy, fever, and cholera; witness what these iron men sometimes had to endure. On one occasion the Architect was driven two hundred miles in twelve hours by a hurricane. One of the most hair-raising voyages was made by an American clipper, called Neptune's Car, on a voyage to San Francisco, in 1856. Her captain, who had come down with brain fever, several thousand miles from port, was blind and deaf. The first officer was under arrest. The ship was brought home under the command of the captain's wife, aged nineteen, who was nicknamed the "Florence Nightingale of the Ocean."

In 1858, on a voyage to Hong Kong, the crew of the California clipper, Golden State, insisting they were not getting enough to eat, mutinied and attacked their officers with hand spikes, killing the first mate. In 1863, the crew of the Asterion were marooned on an island after she sank and had to live on a diet of snakes until they were rescued. In 1872, the Caliph disappeared in the South China Sea, and evidence indicates that she was boarded by Chinese pirates, the crew murdered, and the ship scuttled. Part of the evidence is based on the facts that there was no record of any foul weather at the time of her reported loss and that a couple of years after her mysterious disappearance some of her navigational equipment and chronometers showed up in a Hong Kong "pawn shop."

Regardless of whose flag they sailed under, all clipper ships had one thing in common: their crews were exceedingly tough. A hard, dangerous life, it called for men with iron nerves and strong muscles. The chief mate of one clipper said he could only use men who were able "to jump over the foreyard before breakfast."

Yes, these were truly iron men. But why this willingness to endure such incredible hardship and deprivation? A piece of information here, a piece there, makes the puzzle fit; and the puzzle has a quite simple solution. It was the only way of life these men knew. Just as we accustom ourselves to our environment from childhood, so did they, for almost all of them were sailors from their early youth. The majority of seamen during the days of sail went to sea at the age of nine or ten. Generally driven from homes by dire poverty and starvation, life on board ship wasn't really too terrible a fate for them. There was food to eat, a place to sleep, and a little money to be made. Starting a life at sea at ten, it soon became the only life most of these men really knew. A ship, although strange to us, was their home, their comfort, and their security. Perhaps one would have to walk the decks of a clipper ship on a warm, breathless night in a silent, tropical sea, shimmering like a sheet of steel, listening to the tide sucking round the hull, to understand the great security of the sea compared to the unrest of the land.

I've read stories about old-time sailors who went to sea at such an early age they actually didn't remember their nationality. During wars, their homelands disappeared. With the passage of time, parents died off, families immigrated to the four corners of the earth, leaving nothing for them but their ship. Money was meaningless. They couldn't spend it on board ship and material possessions had no value. They never made enough money, nor were they ever in one place long enough, to acquire any property and have it develop any value. Did you ever see a child put away candy "for a rainy day?" Give him ten cents worth of penny candy, and he'll eat it on the spot. Well, money to sailors was the same; it was just a tool to attain a little fleeting material pleasure during their brief and infrequent stays in port. John Masefield said it — no one could have said it better.

They towed her in to Liverpool, we made the hooker*
fast,

———
*Anchor

Courtesy The Peabody Museum of Salem

Trimming sail in a heavy sea, off the Horn.

And the copper-bound officials paid the crew
And Billy drew his money, but the money didn't last,
For he painted the alongshore blue,—
It was rum for Poll, and rum for Nan, and gin for
    Jolly Jack
He shipped a week later in the clothes upon his
    back,
He had to pinch a little straw, he had to beg a
    sack
To sleep on, when his watch was through,—
    So he did.

from "Hell's Pavement"

William Cock, who shipped as chief officer on the Cutty Sark's 1869/1870 maiden voyage, described the routine on board a clipper thus:

"We were kept hard at it all the time, either making sail or taking it in. It was four hours on and four hours off throughout the passage, and in heavy squalls all hands were called up, so that their rest was broken frequently, whilst in fine weather there was the mending and washing of clothes to be seen to in spare time. There was little time for recreation or for thinking of anything but work."

In order to get the last ounce of speed from a clipper, every available piece of canvas was spread to catch the wind — they called it "cracking on the dimity," dimity being a type of sail cloth. After one trip, a witty crew-hand said that they flew everything but the captain's night shirt. In very bad weather, the safest thing for a ship's captain to do was usually to shorten sail, since a strong enough wind could snap a mast, carry away a yard, or rip a spread of canvas to shreds. But this meant reducing speed, and clipper captains who were "drivers" often took risks. A good "driver" captain liked nothing better than skimming down the South China Sea passage before a strong monsoon with every yard of canvas, that the ship could handle, bent on the yards. He'd take in sail only when he was dead certain that a yard or mast might be carried away, and even then, only at the very last moment. Consequently, in some of the worst weather that man can imagine, sails had to be shortened or new sails bent to replace those torn off the yards. The crew had to scramble aloft in hurricane, cyclone, or full gale, to reef or furl, struggling with hundreds of yards of heavy canvas.

Furling the main sail in a gale: "one hand for yourself and one for the ship."

"A hundred feet above a heaving, pitching deck; soaked through, eyes full of spray, hands numbed with cold, frozen to the marrow of their bones, it was 'one hand for me and one for the ship.'"

Basil Lubbock in his book, *Round the Horn Before the Mast*, describes how a sail was bent on a yard:

> For those who may not know how a square-sail is bent,
> I may perhaps be permitted to give a short explanation: —
> First you have to hoist the sail up by means of a block
> and gantline until the bunt, which is made fast to the
> end of the gantline, is well above the yard — (always
> send up a sail to windward). Then the sail is spread
> along the yard, head up, and the head-earings passed
> by the men at each yardarm. Then the buntlines and
> leech-lines, which are used to clew up the sail, are

clinched. Then you tie the head of the sail to the jackstay, which is an iron bar running along the top of the yard. This is done with rovings, lengths of rope yarn, three or more being passed according to whether the sail is a royal, topgallant, topsail, of course; the sheet and clew-line being shackled on to the clew by the men at the yardarms. The sail is then picked up and furled by means of the gaskets, short ropes made fast to the jackstay, and wound round and round the sail and yard to hold the sail up when furled.

All this is no easy business for two men on each yard-arm and one at the bunt, with the sail dragging and blowing aback and trying to knock you off the foot-ropes, and half a gale of wind in your face.

The old rule on a yard is, "one hand for yourself and one for the ship," which means, hold on with one hand and work with the other. But if you want to get the work done in a case like this, when so shorthanded or in real bad weather, I defy anyone to do much good with only one hand; you soon find yourself using both, extremely dangerous as it is, for the sail has a way of flying up over the yard and hitting you in the face, which, if you have not got fast hold of the backstay, must send you over backwards.

There was plenty of other hard work to be done too, especially on the run into port, when the ship had to be made as smart as possible. The crew had to paint the masts, tar the rigging, oil the decks, fill the seams with white lead and boiling pitch, scour and varnish the wood, polish the brass, and scrub the decks with holystone, a form of pumice. The clipper seamen used to say, "Six days shalt thou labour and do all that thou art able, And on the seventh holystone the decks and scrape the cable."

William Cock of the Cutty Sark further commented: "Whether they ever had time to go ashore or not in the East I hardly remember. I don't think I did. It was hard work all the time. At sea you were racing against everything, and in harbour you were either discharging or taking in cargo."

The life of a sailor generally started as fo'c'sle boy, the lowliest position on board ship. If you were a strong, stout, intelligent-looking chap, there was generally a berth available, for boys were always in demand since they were the pool from which future sailors were drawn. These boys were oft times orphans, and almost always drawn from the very poorest background in the country. As ship's boys they could earn up to ten shillings ($2.50) a month, which for most of them was a fortune. I remember reading the biography of a ship's captain who started his sea life at nine as a fo'c'sle boy "going in at the hawsehole." He mentioned that in the first nine years of his life he had only possessed a total of six pennies, so the wages offered him as a fo'c'sle boy were huge. A boy's needs to ship aboard were simple; his worldly possessions needed to consist of only:

    a pair of shoes — no nails in them
    2 pair of canvas trowsers
    1 pair of cloth trowsers
    2 blue flannel shirts
    1 jacket
    1 straw bed (commonly known amongst sailors as a donkey's breakfast)

The fo'c'sle, home for the able-body seaman. Oft times in heavy seas, it would fill with sea water to the level of the lower bunks.

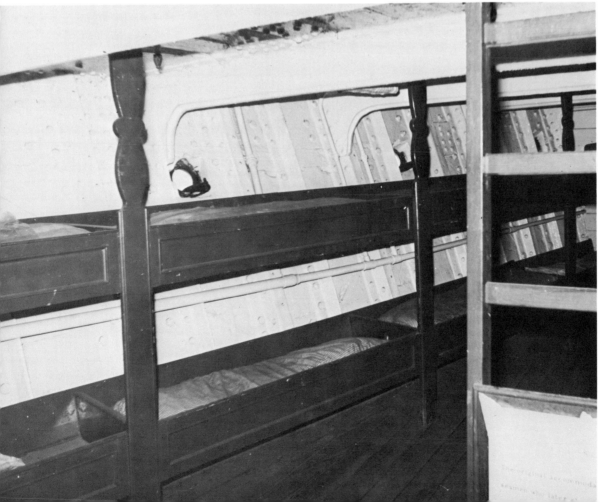

1 blanket and 1 rug
1 knife and 1 tin plate and a spoon

Purchased for about two pounds sterling, even this sum was usually advanced to the boy by the captain and deducted from his wages. As he progressed up the ranks from boy to ordinary seaman, and on then to able body seaman, his needs did not change very much. Perhaps the only other things he might add to his kit during his entire life at sea would be a suit of oilcloth and a pair of seaboots.

His duties as fo'c'sle boy were the most menial: cleaning the heads, keeping the forecastle in order, repairing the sailors' clothes, fetching their food, and giving a hand with deck chores but still keeping out of the way of the work gangs. It was expected that, as part of his duties, he would learn the basic rudiments of the ship: the various parts of the rigging, the locations of sheets and halyards, and the general order of things on board. As a cabin boy, he had basically the same duties except that he also served the captain and took care of the master's simplest needs. "Fetch my cap from below, boy!"

If a boy came from a little money and wanted to prepare for an officer's berth and eventual command, he could often ship as an apprentice for a year or two, after which he would be as competent as most able seamen. His parents would pay the ship owner a premium of up to fifty pounds sterling per voyage to have him signed on to be taught the business of seafaring. He might really be described as an unpaid ordinary seaman: in many ships the apprentices did the lion's share of the work, and plenty of boys whose people had paid good premiums for them spent most of their time scouring decks and paintwork, chipping plates and tarring down, receiving no instruction whatever beyond what they could pick up in the way of seamanship from the petty officers or from senior apprentices.

There might be typically anywhere from five to fifteen apprentices on board a clipper during a passage. This had a major economic effect for ship owners, since the apprentices provided a solid core of free, efficient, and loyal labour plus a continuing supply of new officers. Oftentimes it was a good thing they were there, for more than once, when disaster struck a clipper or her captain, a mate and the apprentices brought their ship to safe harbour.

Promotion was based solely on one's own ability to judge if he could handle the next job up the line, which was ordinary seaman. If in fact, he did get to ship as an ordinary seaman and couldn't perform

The apprentice quarters on the main deck, not much more comfortable than the fo'c'sle.

the expected duties, a mate would usually cut his wages and relegate him to the duties of a "boy." Wages were a considerable step up, for as an ordinary seaman he might command upwards to two pounds sterling. In fact, one reason why seamen were prepared to put up with the terribly difficult life on board clipper ships, was that they received excellent wages. In the 1850s, the Royal Navy paid its able seamen two pounds one shilling sterling a month, while an ordinary seaman received one pound thirteen shilling. (At the then rate of exchange one pound sterling was equivalent to about $5.00.) During the same period, a clipper owner calculated that the wages for his crew of thirty-nine came to one thousand two hundred twenty-four pounds sterling a year, plus one shilling for "victualling" per man per day. Some crews on American packet clippers made twenty-five dollars a month on the

Liverpool to New York run, and it was not unknown for them to get a bonus of fifty dollars each if they won a race against another packet ship.

As an ordinary seaman, generally, he was either not considered to be of sufficient age or strength for an able seaman's berth, or he did not have the necessary experience to assume duties of any major responsibility. However, he was expected to be able to hand reef and steer under ordinary weather conditions, to box the compass, shovel ballast and have an acquaintance with all the standing and running rigging. He was also required to be able to reeve some or all of the studding-sail gear, go aloft and furl sail and send down the mizzen topgallant yard. In his spare time he was expected to learn, from whomever might be willing to teach him, some of the rudiments of navigation. He might be twelve to fourteen years old by now.

The next step up the ladder was that of able seaman. In this capacity he was expected to have a full knowledge of all the rigging, which included any mending, repairing, and refitting of any rigging or portion of it when the occasion demanded. He was also required to have a complete knowledge of steering, reefing, and furling sail. As an able seaman, he was placed in the most important parts of the working ship, such as the fo'c'sle deck, at the main tack, or at the fore and main topmast braces or at either of the lower braces. As a fully responsible able seaman, he worked watch and watch, i.e., four hours on and four hours off, alternating the dog watch of two hours in the afternoon. He worked an average of twelve hours a day, seven days a week for the entire duration of the voyage. At no time did he ever get more than three and a half hours of effective sleep at a stretch. In foul weather he was on call twenty-four hours a day, and could be called out at any time to help the working watch make or take in sail, as the weather demanded, and the captain ordered. The wages for an able seaman were about three pounds sterling a month with quarters and food, but no clothing provided. For most of those who took to the sea, able seaman was the end of the line — a life style they were to follow for the rest of their days, till disease, fever, or the sea itself released them from their self-imposed bondage.

However, for those who really wanted to make a career of the sea, the real learning period was just beginning — the struggle to become master. Young officers would have to master a huge mass of sailing lore, and learn through trial and error all the techniques and tricks of seamanship necessary to sail and navigate a great clipper. They would have to rigidly condition themselves to go without sleep for days on end, while still maintaining at all times perfect judgment of wind, weather, gear, and sea. They would need to become in their own right master-sailmakers, master-riggers, master stevedores and master ship-wrights. During these young years, they would need to develop great leadership ability, steel nerves, a tremendous business sense, and above all, that certain, unique, and indefinable ability to command. The day might certainly come when his decisions and commands alone could mean life or death for his ship and crew. He had therefore to train himself to use this power wisely.

So now our young fo'c'sle boy had to start all over again as second mate, the lowliest officer on board. His wages were generally five pounds sterling per month, and his first and most important duty was supervision of the stowage of cargo. When the ship arrived at her port of discharge, the second mate was expected to know where every package was stowed, and how it was stowed. In many ports of the world where no stevedores were to be found, the ship's crew had to stow and discharge cargo themselves, with the second officer being fully responsible for its transfer. He also had the responsibility of selecting and supervising the proper laying of dunnage, that material which was placed between the skin of the ship and the cargo to prevent the latter from getting damaged.

While at sea his duties included command of the starboard watch when the captain was not on deck. He was expected to know enough navigation to keep the ship's course and distance during his watch, and to correctly enter them on the log slate. If he mastered these and many other duties for a reasonable period of time, with a favorable reference from his captain, he could then stand for his examination for chief officer, or first mate. It was not unusual for young men eighteen to twenty years old to hold a first mate's, or as otherwise called, a Chief Officer's certificate.

In performing his duties as chief officer, he had full command of the ship, when the captain was below or disabled. Complete awareness of his ship's overall condition was imperative, as was his ability to perform every shipboard operation as well, if not better, than any other man aboard. Instantly, and unfailingly, he was required to execute every command of the captain. Wages for a chief officer generally ran eight pounds sterling per month.

When once established as a master, his life was a relatively good one and well paid by the standards of the time, typically two hundred

Courtesy The National Maritime Museum, London

Agreement and account of crew: Cutty Sark's outward passage, London to Sydney, 1875.

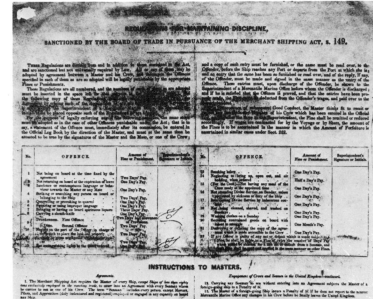

REGULATIONS FOR MAINTAINING DISCIPLINE,

SANCTIONED BY THE BOARD OF TRADE IN PURSUANCE OF THE MERCHANT SHIPPING ACT, s. 149.

No.	OFFENCE	Amount of Fine or Punishment	Superintendent's Signature or Initials	No.	OFFENCE	Amount of Fine or Punishment	Superintendent's Signature or Initials
1	Not being on board at the time fixed by the agreement	Two Day's Pay.		14	Smoking below	One Day's Pay.
2	Not returning on board at the expiration of leave	One Day's Pay.		15	Neglecting to bring up, open out, and air bedding, when ordered	Half a Day's Pay.
3	Insolence or contemptuous language or behaviour towards the Master or any Mate			16	(For the Cook) Not having any meal of the Crew ready at the appointed time	One Day's Pay.
4	Quarrelling or provoking to quarrel	Two Day's Pay.	81	17	Not attending Divine Service on Sunday, when required by the Master of the Ship	One Day's Pay.
5	Striking or assaulting any person on board or belonging to the Ship			18	Interrupting Divine Service by indecorous conduct	One Day's Pay.
6	Bringing or having on board spirituous liquors	One Day's Pay.		19	Not being washed, shaved, and washed on Sundays	One Day's Pay.
7	Carrying a sheath-knife	Three Day's Pay.		20	Washing clothes on a Sunday	One Day's Pay.
8	Drunkenness. First Offence	Two Day's Pay		21	Secreting contraband goods on board with intent to smuggle	One Month's Pay.
9	Ditto. Second Offence	Two Day's Pay.	81	22	Destroying or defacing the copy of the agreement which is made accessible to the Crew	One Day's Pay.
10	Neglect on the part of the Officer in charge of a Watch to place the log line ... properly ...	Two Day's Pay.				
11	Not extinguishing lights at the time ordered					

INSTRUCTIONS TO MASTERS.

Agreements.

1. The Merchant Shipping Act requires the Master of every Ship, except Ships of less than eighty tons exclusively employed in the coasting trade, to enter into an Agreement with every Seaman whom he carries to sea as one of his Crew. The term "Seaman" includes every person except Masters, Pilots, and Apprentices (duly indentured and registered) employed or engaged in any capacity on board any Ship.

2. In order to enable the Seamen to know the contents of the Agreement, the Master at the commencement of the Voyage is bound under a Penalty of 5l. to have a legible copy (omitting the Signatures) placed in an accessible part of the Ship.

...

[additional instructions text largely illegible]

Engagement of Crews and Seamen in the United Kingdom.

...

Ports abroad.

...

Return to the United Kingdom.

...

JACKSON & CO. 57 CLIPPER ROPE AND THE CUTTY SARK.

PRINTED IN ENGLAND.

Ship: Cutty Sark — AGREEMENT No. 7818

PARTICULARS OF DISCHARGE

				Date, Place, and Cause of leaving this Ship, or of Death						No.
				Date	Place	Cause				
						Hay is	Commander			1
8	8	2	81	25/10/75	London	disch	23/28	Wm Cooper	B S	2
8	8		81	24/10/75	do	do		Joseph Clay	B S	3
6	6	3	81	20/10/75	do	do	11/74	Robert Mottatt	B S	4
4.10	4.10	25	81	22/10/75	do	do		William Hall	B S	5
4.15	4.15	276	81	22/10/75	do	do		John Brooks	B S	6
4.10	4.10		81	27/10/75	do	do		John Barret	B S	7
3.5	3.5		81	14/9/74		Drowned accidentally		Albert	Apl	8
3.5	3.5		81	20/10/75	London	disch	15/24	Sinclair	B S	9
3.5	3.5		81	20/10/75	do	do	26.62	Henry Scott	B S	10
3.5	3.5		81	20/10/75	do	do		Medal Oak	B S	11
3.5	3.5		81		Sydney	Deserted		No appearance	B S	12
3.5	3.5		81	20/10/75	London	disch		W Anderson	B S	13
3.5	3.5		81		Sydney	Deserted		No appearance	B S	14
3.5	3.5		81	22/10/75	London	disch		Richard Williams	B S	15
3.5	3.5		81	22/10/75	do	do		H S Davis	B S	16
3.5	3.5		81	20/10/75	do	do		George Jeffries	B S	17
3.5	3.5		81	22/10/75	do	do		David Deans	B S	18
3.5	3.5		81	22/10/75	do	do		Frank Fenton	B S	19
3.5	3.5		81		Sydney	Deserted		No appearance	B S	20

the Ship," then "H.M.S. Beware," and the other Cause of leaving the Ship should be briefly stated thus, "Discharged," "Deserted," "Left Sick," "Died."
[Sixteen Pages.]

pounds sterling a year. Fringe benefits allowed him to carry on trade, to a limited extent, for his own account. A resourceful captain, therefore, could live well and might retire with a comfortable income. In fact, many captains who retired from the sea with their accumulated earnings were actually able to acquire ships of their own, or a partnership in one, and thus join the ranks of the shipowners.

The area of the poop was generally considered the private domain of the captain, and from here he was able to conduct his own private affairs. Many captains, who took passengers aboard, could pocket their fares. Then, too, if trade with Cathay was conducted on specialty items, such as liquor and millinery, and as in the case of Captain Woodget of the Cutty Sark, a very profitable business in purebred collies, these monies were also added to his personal coffers. The captains of most clippers ran a concession or "slop chest" as it was called, where once a week all aboard could purchase such items as tobacco, soap, matches, and work clothes. Any purchases would be charged to the seaman's wage, and deducted from it when they were paid at the end of the voyage. After settling their "slop chest" account, most sailors had pitifully little to show for a year at sea.

So it was that a successful clipper captain had to be an excellent business man and trader. His business decisions on what cargo to carry to which ports of call, and his talent in negotiating the most favorable freight rates could make, for the ship owner, the difference between a profitable or losing voyage. On the return trip from China many clipper captains transported rare silks, rugs, spices, and choice teas back to London, where they were sold at a mighty handsome profit for himself.

Still in all, it was a terribly rugged life for all aboard. Living conditions, apart from the captain's quarters, were primitive. Available food was unbelievably bad, even by the standards of those days. The standard daily ration set by the Board of Trade for each man on a typical clipper in the tea trade during the 1870s, exclusive of the daily ration of lime or lemon juice and sugar, was as follows:

1 lb. bread daily, usually in the form of hard tack (hard biscuits)
1½ lb. salt beef on Sunday, Tuesday, Thursday, and Saturday
1¼ lb. salt pork on Monday, Wednesday, and Friday
½ lb. flour on Monday, Wednesday, and Friday
¼ pt. dried peas on Tuesday, Thursday, and Saturday
½ lb. rice once a week
¼ oz. tea daily

The galley: on this cast-iron wood burning stove all the crew's meals were prepared, when the galley was dry enough to light a fire.

12 oz. sugar weekly
2 qts. water daily for drinking and washing

Clipper crews really had to have strong stomachs. With no refrigeration on ships in those days the food was almost always anything but fresh. Cooking in a small galley in a heavy sea was far from easy, and some really peculiar concoctions were dished up. Biscuits were sometimes put in a canvas bag and beaten up with an iron bar, then cooked with bits of meat. The result became known as "cracker hash." Recipes known as "dog's body" and "dandyfunk" were served, consisting of biscuits mixed with molasses and salt pork and other ingredients.

A former clipper captain, writing his autobiography, described what the bread ration in 1898 consisted of; one who would have really had to live through it to so aptly be able to describe it.

According to the Board of Trade scale, each man was given a ration of one pound of "bread" per day. This usually consisted of five hard-baked biscuits. Each biscuit had forty-two holes in one side, to let the

heat out of the center and make it as hard as concrete.
The other side was smooth. The biscuits for the day
were kept in a wooden box called a "bread barge,"
which was hung up to the deckhead in the half deck and
fo'c'sle, to prevent rats from getting at it.
Twice a week our German cook baked soft bread, from
white flour. These loaves were known as "rooties,"
which I believe is a Hindustani word, adopted from
the olden days of the East India Company's merchantmen.
After we had reached the tropics, the rooties
became inedible, as the yeast went mouldy. One of
our sailors complained to the cook of this. "You
couldn't cook hot water for a barber's shop!" he said.
German Charlie promptly hit the sailor on the point of
the jaw and knocked him out. "By shiminy," he
bellowed, "you vill eat der rotten rooties or go mitout!"
As the voyage proceeded, the ship's biscuits became weevily. The
weevils hid in the forty-two holes.
The game was to thump the biscuits on the deck, with the
holed side downward, to knock the weevils out. Paddy
Murphy scorned to do this. "Eat the weevils and all,"
he advised me. "Sure and they're fresh meat."

During a long voyage in hot weather, butter, when it was on board,
would melt and reset itself several times. Then, too, small black beetles,
called weevils, got into the rice and spoiled a lot of appetites. The
most unpleasant things, however, were maggots, which grew especially
fat in flour. Holding maggot races at mealtimes became a popular
pastime. Hens were also taken on board many of the clippers, but
since they were kept mostly in coops, the few eggs which they did
lay, besides being quite tasteless, were for the exclusive use of the
officers.

Salt beef and pork, the mainstays of a clipper crew's diet, were
stored in "harness casks" lashed to the poop-deck rail. The daily ration
was weighed out from these harness casks, which was then whacked
out from the cook's galley, after being cooked. The day's ration became
known as "the whack" and the term was applied to the issue of water
as well as food.

Depending upon the generosity of the owner or the mood of the
captain, sometimes a few pigs were shipped for fresh meat on the out-

ward pasage. On the homeward passage, a clipper captain might occasionally stop at Anjer in order to lay in a fresh supply of fruits, meat, and vegetables. However, none of them lasted very long in the heat of the tropics, so it pretty quickly was back to "salt horse."

Each day's meals were constantly monotonous. Breakfast was burgoo — a watery porridge with the flavoring of weevils. Dinner, the main meal which was served at noon, was boiled salt meat and hard tack. Sometimes it was served with pea soup so thick that it could actually be cut like a pie and eaten off of the point of a knife. Salt beef and pork were quite tolerable so long as they were smothered in pickle, but when the pickle ran out the meat tasted, according to one sailor, like "a bit of old ship stewed in her own bilge water." Supper was leftovers scraped together from the other two meals. By law the ship owner or captain was not required to issue any further rations for the duration of the cruise, other than those agreed to in the "Agreement and Account of Crew."

There is an old sea story about a young seaman who, when he first went on the daily rations, began to feel famished every day. One day he told a fellow seaman how hungry he was. "Never mind," he said, "you can always get a good feed o' wind puddin's." Thinking he had missed something, he asked "What are they?" "Put y'r 'ead over the t'gallant rail," the old salt said, "and take a few good gasps o' ozone. Them's wind puddin's!"

Samuel Johnson said, "No man will be a sailor who has contrivance enough to get himself into a jail; for being in a ship is being in a jail with the chance of being drowned. A man in jail has more room, better food and commonly better company." I wonder if there may not have been more truth than fancy in that remark.

VI

"WITH HER ROYALS SET AND A BONE IN HER MOUTH"

In the grey of the coming on of night
She dropped the tug at the Tuskar light,
'N the topsails went to the topmast head
To a chorus that fairly awoke the dead.
She trimmed her yards and slanted South
With her royals set and a bone in her mouth.
JOHN MASEFIELD, from "The Yarn of the *Loch Achray*"

Scooting down the Channel, under a great press of sail, the bow waves boiling and thrashing into sprays, jib boom dipping to the swells, the Cutty Sark slanted South for Cathay, the first tack on a million mile voyage.

But all was not well. Captain Moodie was plagued with rigging problems, faulty iron work and unusually light weather. The rigging and iron works problems were anticipated, but not the light weather. Any new ship will have its problems, stays and shrouds stretch and retuning the rigging becomes an ever continuing chore. Sheets and halliards chafe, fittings snap, purchases and falls two-block. Captain and crew alike had to be ever alert, for what "couldn't happen," invariably "did."

The weather, too, presented problems. In the doldrums, the whole week's run, from March 10th to the 16th, totaled only four hundred thirty-five miles. The frustrations were beginning to show on Captain Moodie, for on March 26th he entered into the log:

"Lat. 26°26'S., Long. 23°47'W., Course S.21°W.
Distance 15 miles. Calm! Calm! Calm! Sea like
a mirror.

All things being considered, the Cutty Sark still made most accept-

"Thermopylae Racing the Cutty Sark," from an oil painting by John R.C. Spurling.

able outward passage of one hundred four days to Shanghai, and a few good runs "to boot" as shown from the abstract of her log:

> April 14 — Lat. 44°18'S. Long. 47°8'E. Course east. Distance 360 miles. Winds North, fresh. P.M. moderate.
>
> April 15 — Lat. 44°25'S., Long. 53°22'E. Course S. 88½°E. Winds North to W.N.W., fresh and rainy. Distance by log 343 miles.
>
> April 18 — Lat. 42°17'S., Long. 73°51'E., Course N 79°E. Distance 336 miles. Winds N.N.E. to S.E., fresh gales and dry weather.

Only five other clippers made better passages: Lahloo — ninety-eight days, Sir Lancelot — ninety-eight days, Taeping — one hundred two, Kaisow — ninety-nine, and the Wylo — one hundred three days. The outward passage of 1869/1870, however, was not without disaster for the clippers. The beautiful Spindrift was wrecked on the Dungeness when the pilot mistook a star for Dungeness station light, and Blackadder was dismasted and almost lost when, in a violent gale, her maintop chains parted, carrying away both the main mast and the mizzen. However the Blackadder finally did manage to arrive in Shanghai on December 11, 1870, two hundred sixty-two days out of London. Interestingly enough, the Cutty Sark in her fifty-three years of sailing all the oceans of the world was dismasted only twice, first under the British flag due to the carelessness of her mate, and then under the ownership of the Portuguese, as the "Ferreira."

In Shanghai, the "Cutty" loaded the first of many tea cargos, 1,305,812 pounds, at a top freight rate of three pounds ten shillings. Only two other already proven clippers, the Taeping and Serica, were able to contract freight at the same rate; an indication of the great esteem which shippers held for this new challenger.

Holds were cleaned and fumigated, and the bamboo matting dunnage was laid in. The tea chests, literally, were "screwed into the holds;" loaded into every conceivable corner of the ship, even stuffed under bunks. Of course, every chest carried in the poop was the captain's personal property, an opportunity to turn a few extra pounds profit for himself.

Then with the loading completed on June 26, 1870, the Cutty Sark slipped her mooring, braced her yards, and with the China coast fading into a thin, blurred, grey line, set herself down the dangerous South China Sea passage, homeward bound.

Unfortunately, however, under the command of Captain Moodie, who was her Master on the 1870, '71, and '72 passages, the "Cutty" was never to realize her tremendous potential as the fastest ship ever to sail the seas. This was due to the fact that Moodie, though an extremely competent ship master and a superb navigator, was by no stretch of the imagination a "driver." To Moodie, the safety of the ship, crew, and cargo came first, and he never would take an unnecessary risk to clip a day off a sailing record. The "Cutty" was like a thoroughbred, tightly reined in and never given her head to really fly. It would be years before she was to realize her full potential.

To really understand the highly conservative nature of Captain Moodie, we must follow him down the China Sea to Anjer during the 1870 homeward passage. The real clipper "drivers," like Captain Kemball, of the Thermopylae, hugged the shoal China coast in order to work westward of the dangerous Paracels and thus be able to pick up the prevailing land breezes and the southerly set of the current off the Cochin China coast. From there, he would run down east of Natuna Besar through the Gaspar Strait to Anjer. Moodie departed Shanghai June 25, 1870, and after clearing the Formosa Strait, elected to sail eastward of the Pratas Island and work South against the wind. After being becalmed for eighteen hours north of the Scarborough Shoal he finally worked over towards the Cochin China coast in order to pass South of Macclesfield Bank and shape a course between the Natunas. He kept clear of the Borneo coast because of the shoals and

Courtesy National Maritime Museum

George Moodie, the Cutty Sark's first Captain and supervisor of her construction.

Another view of Whampoa in the 1840s.

hidden rocks and consequently was unable to take advantage of the land breezes off the shore. Finally, instead of taking the tricky rock strewn Gaspar Strait passage, he again elected the safer but much longer passage through the Carimata Strait between Billiton Island and Borneo. Finally on August 2, thirty-seven days out from Shanghai, the Cutty Sark dropped her hook off Anjer. Thermopylae made the passage from Foochow to Anjer in twenty-eight days. However we must keep in mind the fact that Foochow is about four hundred fifty nautical miles closer to Anjer than Shanghai.

For the remainder of the Cutty Sark's maiden voyage, after departing Anjer, she was generally beset with foul winds, as abstracted from Captain Moodie's log:

Aug — 6 "This ship is apparently doomed to light winds."
Aug — 12 "Sails clashing against the masts."
Aug — 17 "Nearly calm."
Aug — 22 "Light baffling airs."

She finally made the Beachy Head Landfall on October 12, one hundred nine days pilot to pilot.

Still in all, of the thirty-four tea clippers of any note involved in the 1870 tea passage, only twelve beat the "Cutty's" time. Of these the Leander and Lahloo both departed China on October 12, 1870, and arrived off Deal in a dead heat on January 17, 1871, ninety-eight days out. Yet, the Cutty Sark managed soundly to beat many of the top-rated clippers of the day including Taeping, Titania, Serica, Taitsing, and Forward Ho. Even though she did not have the best of luck on this maiden voyage, both Willis and Moodie knew they really had a real challenger, and given the right set of circumstances she could beat the Thermopylae. The test was to be soon at hand.

The outward passage of 1871, Captain Moodie again in command, was a very fine one indeed. Departing the London River on November 8, 1870, in tow of the tug MacGregor, she anchored off Shanghai at 11:00 a.m. February 6, 1871, a ninety day passage. One interesting abstract from her log indicates just how good Moodie's passage was up to this point in time:

> Jan 24 — Lat. 8°32′ Long. 125′S. Course N, 71°E. Distance 95. A light breeze from westward. Steering towards the Ombai Passage between Timor and Ombai Island. Two ships in night, which proved to be Titania and Sir Harry Parks, former from London to Shanghai, latter London to Hong Kong. Another ship coming up astern which proves to be Taeping, from London for Shanghai. This ship left London 17 days before us, we took her berth after she was loaded. Noon, calms and baffling airs. East-end of Ombai, bears N.E. 13 miles. Currents by W. ¼ W., 11 miles."

The Cutty Sark, having arrived too early to start loading the new teas, busied herself in coastal trading along the China coast between Shanghai and Bangkok. When the teas finally did come down river, Moodie had difficulties finding good freight rates. Finally he did manage to load a cargo at three pounds sterling. On September 4, 1871, then in company with Ariel, the "Cutty" departed for London. An informal race between the two was in the making. The two ships, very early in the race, lost sight of each other, probably because of the safe course that Moodie set down the middle passage of the South China Sea. Moodie took thirty-two days to reach Anjer with Ariel nowhere in sight. After some rough weather around the Cape of Good Hope, Moodie scooted up the Atlantic, arriving at North Foreland one hundred eight days out of Shanghai. To the surprise of Captain and crew alike, the Ariel had not arrived and had not been sighted. Ariel finally did arrive a week later.

Now, the year was 1872 and John Willis was to finally get his dearest wish, to pit the Cutty Sark against the Thermopylae. As a result of some of the excellent times she had logged in the 1870 and 1871 passages, he felt confident that his Cutty Sark could beat her rival, Thermopylae. The test was at hand for both ships were in Shanghai for the first time, loading tea together. Tension was running high and the air was electric with the excitement of the race. Both Captains and crews were confident of victory. Early in the morning of June 18, 1872, the Cutty Sark crossed the Woosung bar at the mouth of the Shanghai with Thermopylae close behind. A thick, soupy fog, carried in on a southwesterly, forced both ships to anchor, however. As the fog lifted, from time to time, both ships cautiously began to work their way towards the sea. Finally the fog moved out. The Cutty Sark dropped her pilot on June 21 and picked up the monsoon, which started blowing strong and freshened into a gale. By June 24, she was well into the Formosa Strait with Amoy abeam, and Thermopylae in sight. In a torrential rainfall the two separated from each other, but by June 26, with Hong Kong abeam, they again sighted one another. On the 28th, the two ships were still in full view of each other, with Thermopylae six miles to windward. The Macclesfield Bank was left to leeward by both ships on the 29th. On July 1 they again parted company and on the second of July Moodie fixed his position at Lat. 14° 17′N., Long. 111°17′E., which put him a hundred odd miles off of the Cochin China coast, about abeam of present day Qui Nhon, South Viet Nam. Moodie now set a course down the South China Sea picking up the Cape Sirik, Sarawak, landfall on July 8. Then, instead of taking the shorter Api passage, he tacked westward leaving Natuna to leeward. On July 15 the Cutty Sark was at Lat. 108°18′E on the equator in the vicinity of Direction Rock, where once again the Thermopylae was sighted bearing about eight miles N.N.W. She led Thermopylae through the Stolz Channel in the Gaspar Strait. Due to more favorable slant of the wind Thermopylae beat the Cutty Sark through the Gaspar Strait and passed Anjer about one and one-half hours ahead of her. The Cutty Sark arrived July 19 at 6:00 a.m. Both ships were twenty-eight days out from Shanghai and Moodie, as cautious as he was, had begun to show the stuff of which the "Cutty" was made. For although he took the safer and longer route through the South China Sea, he still managed to equal Captain Kemball's time.

On went the contest, and by July 26 the Cutty Sark, passing Keeling Island, had a three mile lead on the Thermopylae. Now, having picked up the E.S.E. trade winds, the Cutty Sark was really in her element, and her tremendous driving power began to tell. Pressing on every yard of canvas the spars would carry, she literally flew across the waters and she never again saw Thermopylae for the remainder of the race. By August 7 the Cutty Sark was some four hundred miles ahead of Thermopylae. On the 10th of August Moodie ran into squally weather which proceeded to get worse as the days wore on. The wind blew like thunder beating her, thrashing her, tearing the tops off mountainous waves and flinging spray and foam like millions of flashing steel darts. Screaming squalls tore her fore and main lower topsails to shreds. Then after days of unmerciful pounding, by millions of tons of booming seas, disaster struck!

> "August 15 — Lat. 34°26′S Long. 28°1′E. At 6:00 a.m. a heavy sea struck the rudder and carried it away from the trunk downwards. Noon, wind more moderate, tried a spar over the stern but would not steer the ship. Thereupon began construction of a jury rudder with a spare spar 70 feet long."

With this cold and unemotional log entry by Captain Moodie began one of the truly incredible feats of seamanship in the annals of maritime history.

Rather than put in a South African port, which was not Moodie's way nor the way of any clipper captain worth his salt, he set to fashioning a jury rudder from spare spars and ironwork and fitting this jury rig onto the crippled "Cutty," battered by mountainous seas, and totally incapable of maneuvering except by the trim of the sails. Here are his own words as taken from his private log describing this Herculean task:

> The making of the rudder was, however, the only simple part of it, the connecting it to the post and securing it to the ship so that it would work and be of sufficient strength for use when placed was the most difficult part of the job. The connection was made by putting eye-bolts in both rudderposts and rudder, and placing them so that the one would just clear the other; a large bolt (an awning stanchion) was then passed through them and clenched on both ends; in this way we had five eye-bolts in each, locked with two strong bolts which would bear considerable weight. The securing of the whole to the ship was of the next importance and it was soon apparent that this could not be done in the way usually recom-

mended, viz., by placing chains along the ship's bottom and leading into the hawse pipes; in the first place, the Cutty Sark is too sharp for chain to lie along the keel, and in the next place the length of the ship is too great, it would be difficult to bind the post tightly to the vessel owing to the great length of chain. I therefore concluded to take both the guys into the after mooring pipe, fitting the lower one with a bridle under the keel, 16 feet from the heel of the ship, so that from the post to the bridle there was a little down-pull which prevented post and rudder from rising. The next thing to be done was to get the steering gear secure to the rudder, for the trunk was too small to admit anything but the false sternpost, which came about 2½ feet above the deck, and being wedged round formed a good support. The steering gear had therefore to be secured to the back of the rudder and led to a spar placed across the ship, about 15 feet before the taff-rail, which led the steering chains clear of the counter, and then inboard to the wheel. Of course all the gear was attached to both rudder and post before they were put over the stern. Having a small model of the ship I took all the measurements for the chains by that, which enabled me to place them pretty near the truth.

The abstract from the ship's log tells what Moodie himself wouldn't tell; the weather conditions under which he and the crew had to work to install the temporary rudder:

Aug 16 — Lat. 34°13′S., Long. 28°24′E. Light winds from South. p.m., strong breeze from E.N.E. Constructing jury rudder and sternposts as fast as possible.

Aug 17 — Lat. 34°43′S., Long. 28°28′E. Strong winds from east to E.S.E. Constructing jury rudder and sternpost.

Aug 18 — Lat. 35°58′S., Long. 28°11′E., Strong winds from E.N.E. Constructing jury rudder and sternpost.

Aug 19 — Lat. 34°51′S., Long. 27°58′E. Strong winds from N.E. Constructing jury rudder and sternpost.

Aug 20 — Lat. 34°38′S., Long. 27°36′E. Light wind from westward. Noon, strong westerly breeze and clear. About 2 p.m. shipped jury rudder and sternpost, a difficult job as there was a good deal of sea on.

*The "jury rig" rudder installed by Captain Moodie during the famous Cutty
Sark/Thermopylae race. Photographed in dry dock in 1872.*

The enormity of rigging a jury rudder in high seas can be appreciated when one compares the size of the rudder with the van in the upper right of the photo.

The jury rudder gave away again on September 20, after continual pounding by the seas up the South Atlantic, but even though he was running desperately short of supplies to repair it, Moodie did in fact manage the repair and on the 21st it was lowered into position. Basil Lubbock, in his *Log of the Cutty Sark*, further describes the procedure as follows: "As soon as the rudder was dropped over the stern the sails were filled, and the ship gathered headway the whole contrivance streamed away astern. The sails were then laid aback and the rudder hauled close up to the trunk, the weight of the chains and wires sinking it sufficiently. As soon as the Cutty Sark began to gather sternway, the slack of the guys was got in, the heel of the rudder sinking in the process, so that the head was easily hauled up through the trunk." It sounds so easy, but here was two hundred twenty feet of ship carrying over one million pounds of cargo, no helm and the entire maneuver accomplished by the trim of the sails alone. Try it sometime!

The Cutty Sark reached Gravesend at 9:00 p.m. on the 18th of October, one hundred twenty-two days out from Shanghai.

Considering the fact that she lost five days, at the Cape, fitting the jury rudder and could not exceed eight knots up the Atlantic, for fear of having the temporary rudder torn off again. There was no question as to who, on balance, won the race.

It didn't help the case of Captain Kemball of the Thermopylae any, for when Moodie claimed he was four hundred miles ahead of Thermopylae when he lost his rudder and offered to present his log to prove it, Kemball refused to produce his own log-book. It's interesting to further note that the entire time Kemball was at sea he refused to let any of his officers or crew know the ship's position. The shipping world agreed with Moodie and declared the Cutty Sark the winner.

Captain Moodie resigned his command at the end of the voyage and joined the State Line of Glasgow as master of a steamer. In 1873, Willis put Captain F. W. Moore, out of his Blackadder, in command. At the end of one round trip passage, Moore retired from the sea and was replaced by Captain Tiptaft, out of Willis' Merse, who commanded her from 1874 till his untimely death in the Orient in 1878. Neither Moore nor Tiptaft were clipper "drivers" and the "Cutty" was still waiting to "show her colors." The chief mate under Tiptaft, J. S. Wallace, took command upon the latter's death and here was a master who was things Moodie, Moore, and Tiptaft were not. He was exceptionally well liked by officers and crew alike, with a pleasant word for everybody. Friendly and full of high spirits, he had qualities seldom found in

Chart of the English Channel.

clipper captains of the day. Wallace was particularly keen on the apprentices and rather than treat them like unpaid hands, took the time and effort to further their nautical training and education. But above all things, Wallace was the "driver" that the Cutty Sark needed. As soon as he took command in 1878 he made a brilliant run down the China Sea; Shanghai to Anjer in only sixteen days.

Wallace knew his trade well, was confident of his own ability, was sure of the Cutty Sark; certain of the rigging, the equipment and sails. But he was also too late, for by 1879, clippers had just about disappeared from the China tea trade. While sixty clippers loaded tea in 1869, ten years later with steamships firmly in control of the tea trade, only seven were able to get a tea cargo for London and then at average freight rate of only 30 shillings. The China clipper was finished, and the days of racing home to London with the first of the new season's teas were over.

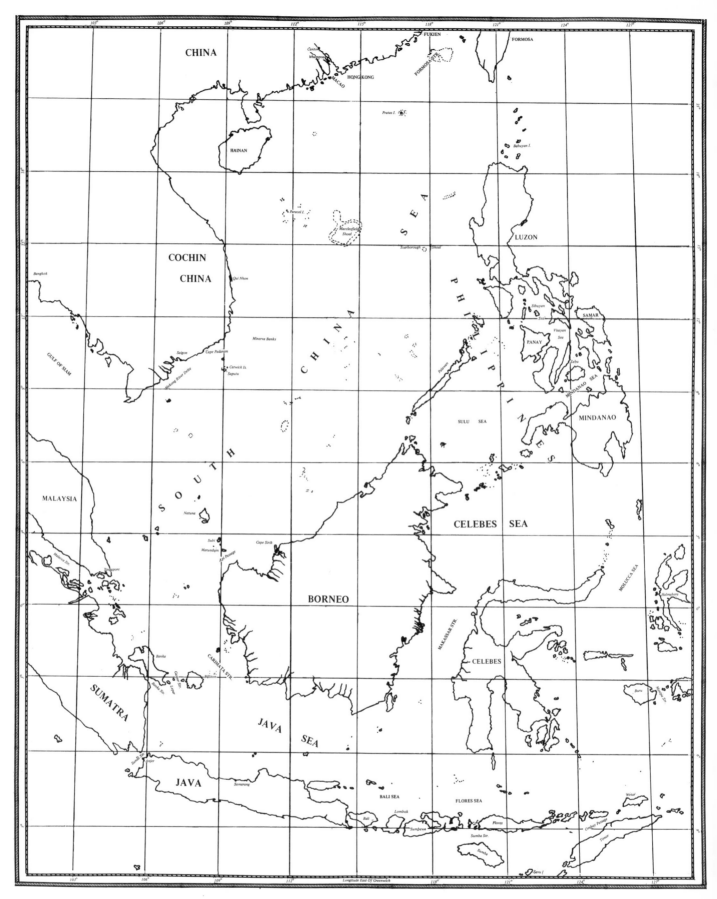

Chart of the South China Sea.

VII

JUST TRAMPING AROUND

We're just tramping around,
With no place special bound.
Is the next port of call Woochow?
It's a rotten life on a' scow.
The wind and waves set our course,
Pressed on by the great sea's force.
Till the end of my dying day,
I'm doomed to drift the current's way.

Author

Wallace could not get a tea cargo for the 1879 homeward passage and rather than take general cargo, and there wasn't much of that, at thirty shillings, he sailed for Manila loading jute and sugar for New York, arriving January 12, 1880, one hundred eleven days out. Upon arriving in New York, Wallace received orders to sail for London and leaving New York on February 14, 1880, in a raging gale, determined to break the Atlantic crossing record, he quickly proceeded to lose his foresail and lower and upper topsails. But driver that he was he continued on, carrying all the sail the "Cutty" could handle and arrived at Deal nineteen days out from New York.

John Willis was by now convinced the tea trade had come to an end and that the Cutty Sark would have to be content with delivering general cargo wherever chance and the opportunity for profit would direct. So it came about that the Cutty Sark was contracted in the spring of 1880 to deliver Welsh coal to the United States Navy in Yokohama. Loading her cargo in Penarth and shipping a less than desirable crew of mixed nationals, Wallace departed for the Far East on June 4th, 1880, on a cruise that Basil Lubbock described as "A Hell Ship Voyage."

The first mate, John Anderson, was extremely unpleasant, hard driving, and considered by the crew as a bucko mate — a nautical expression describing a bully and blusterer. It wasn't long before Anderson and one of the seamen, a John Francis, were going at it hot and heavy. Tensions ran high between Anderson and the crew. Strangely enough, the crew held Francis in very little regard, considering him to be an incompetent sailor and a trouble maker and a lazy lout. But here was a typical case of those under orders banding together and presenting a united front against authority. On the night of July 11, 1880, Anderson gave a series of orders to Francis, who was on the foc's'le head, which he refused to obey. Enraged, Anderson flew forward to discipline Francis, who apparently grabbed one of the capstan bars and threatened Anderson who, in a blind rage wrested the bar from Francis and brained him with it. Three days later he died and was buried at sea.

This entire incident had a terrible effect on Wallace who, for some unknown reason, rather than let the law take its course, took things into his own hands. We'll never know why — perhaps he knew the type of character Francis was, perhaps he was all intent on protecting a fellow officer, perhaps he felt because Anderson was considered a bucko he would not get fair treatment in the courts. Joseph Conrad, in *The Secret Sharer*, which was based on this incident, might have had some specific insight into the situation for he constantly referred to the murderer as "my double." But whatever the reason or reasons, Wallace, on arriving at Anjer, contrived to have Anderson smuggled aboard an American ship heading for California. This action almost resulted in mutiny, with the crew refusing to weigh anchor, and it was only with the aid of his trusted apprentices and officers that the Cutty Sark was able to make sail. By now, tension and great anxiety had overtaken Wallace; fear of an official investigation making him responsible for the mate's escape and the certainty of having his certificate suspended drove Wallace deeper and deeper into a state of gross depression. On the fourth day after leaving Anjer, Wallace, after asking if the second mate were on deck, climbed on to the taffrail and dropped off the stern into the shark infested water. Thus ended the life of a fine sailing master, a man always well regarded by owners, fellow officers, and crew alike. The fathomless sea had claimed another victim.

But the Cutty Sark's trials were not over yet. Nay, they had hardly begun. With the captain and chief officer gone, command fell to an incompetent second mate. Knowing his limitations, he arranged, through orders from Willis still unaware of the killing or the escape of the mate, to have a Dutch pilot bring the Cutty Sark to Singapore.

Her coal cargo was unloaded and the command transferred to Captain Bruce, who at the time was first mate of Willis' Hallowe'en. A worse master couldn't be chosen. In fact, it is reported that when Willis asked Captain Fowler of the Hallowe'en if Bruce were capable of command, Fowler, hating Bruce with a blind passion and seeing an opportunity to get rid of him, once and for all, quickly responded, "Yes, by all means."

Other than being a competent navigator, nothing else good could be said about him. He was a coward, hypocrite, drunkard, and bully. Terrified of landfalls, incompetent in carrying sail, unable to judge wind, life on board became a "circus," as the apprentices called it. After the coal cargo was unloaded at Singapore, Bruce, under orders and in ballast, sailed for Calcutta in search of freight. Needless to say,

Courtesy National Maritime Museum

Photo of the Cutty Sark in midocean, ghosting along.

Bruce feared the Hooghly River and proceeded, unlike most clipper captains, to have the Cutty Sark towed to Calcutta where she laid at her mooring for four months. Finally she did get a cargo of tea, the first from India, mail, castor oil, and jute for Australia. The Cutty Sark still had a reputation for speed and was not forgotten as a crack tea clipper. However, there was constant tension between crew and officers, and morale was at a low ebb. Bruce was totally incapable of command and the crew knew it. No one seemed to care. Upon arriving in Australia, she loaded coal for Shanghai in company with Blackadder and Hallowe'en. A race to the Woosing bar could have been in the making, but the crew would have no part of it.

Disgust, lack of confidence in Bruce, and constant hazing by the mate had driven the crew close to mutiny. Two more despicable characters than Bruce and the mate couldn't be imagined. To make matters worse, after unloading their coal and moving down to the anchorage, most of the crew contracted cholera. The yellow flag, plague on board, was flown from the truck and the Cutty Sark went into three weeks quarantine, two crew men died, and one apprentice was so weakened that he was permanently removed from the ship. One would think that this was enough for any ship, but there was more to come. Orders arrived to proceed to Zebu and load a jute cargo for New York. Even the passage from Shanghai to Zebu was not without incident. Bruce lost his nerve in the shoal-strewn Mindanao Sea and the mate had to take command. In October, 1881, the Cutty Sark finally made the Zebu anchorage and loaded her jute cargo. A course was set across the Sulu Sea, down the South China Sea through the Gaspar Strait to Anjer. Upon passing Anjer, Bruce and the steward got "roaring drunk" and almost wrecked the Cutty Sark. Although drunk too, the mate quickly realized that to leave Bruce in command would spell disaster for the ship and himself. So he continued to ply him with liquor till Bruce was totally stupified and passed out. Two days later captain, mate, and steward were sufficiently sobered up to proceed on their course to Cape Town, but now food was in short supply, due to Bruce's oversight in not ordering enough at Zebu, and the crew had to go on half rations. A seaman was lost overboard; food had to be begged from a passing ship in the South Atlantic. After passing through the doldrums, rations were drastically cut again and food begged from a passing British warship. Upon arrival in New York, the second mate forced an investigation of the Captain and mate who, when the evidence was all in, were discharged and had their certificates suspended.

Three very rare photographs of the great Bay of Bengal cyclone.

Murder, suicide, plague, drunkenness, men lost at sea, starvation, and the Cutty Sark survived but just survived, still not showing the tremendous potential and power that Hercules Linton had designed into the finely sculptured lines of this beautiful clipper.

It is not too difficult to imagine the consternation of Willis upon hearing all the incredible details of this hell-ship voyage. I imagine he gave more than a passing thought to disposing of the Cutty Sark. She never really made her mark in the tea trade for which she was built, and now that business was about at an end. She couldn't seem to earn her keep as a tramp clipper, and the last series of events during 1880 and 1881 must have strained Willis' patience and good business sense taut as a banjo string. But something had to be done because she was due to load a cargo of case oil (kerosene) for the Far East. John Willis must have had some faith left in her so he transferred Captain E. Moore out of his Blackadder to the Cutty Sark, and with Moore came most of the Blackadder's compliment. On May 4, 1882, with 26,816 cases of case-oil, she departed for Samarang. This was a tremendous load to carry, over two million pounds, considering the almost derelict condition she was in as a result of Bruce's mismanagement. Sails, running rigging, and most of her gear was in a terrible

Courtesy National Maritime Museum

Captain E. Moore, who took command after the tragic voyage under Wallace and Bruce.

state of disrepair, and Willis was not about to pour any more money into the Cutty Sark. But, Moore managed to make Samarang on August 20 after a most trying sail. He was afraid to push her because of frayed gear and worn-out canvas, and he did in fact take his toll of sails. After unloading in Samarang, she sailed in ballast for Madras, loading one hundred tons of redwood and twenty-three hundred ten bags of jaggery, a coarse, dark brown sugar made by evaporating the sap of various kinds of palms and not a very pleasant cargo to carry since, under the pressure of bag upon bag, it leaked a thick molasses-like sludge into the bilge which had to be washed down and pumped out daily, a two to three hour chore on the pumps. One crewman described it as "looking like bags of thick black mud and almost as nice to handle." She then proceeded to Bimlipatam arriving on January 8, 1883, loading six thousand two hundred forty bags of myrobalans, a dried plum-like fruit used in dying, tanning and ink-making and four thousand one hundred sixty-three buffalo horns, thence on to Coconado Bay to complete her cargo, taking on another four thousand seven hundred eighty-one bags of myrobalans and one hundred fifteen bales of deer horns. Departing Coconado on January 31, she was off the Cape of Good Hope March 19, the Lizard on May 31 and reached the London docks on June 2, after three years of tramping round the world.

Still under the command of Captain Moore, she departed in July for Australia with general cargo (see Appendix) arriving at Newcastle, New South Wales, in October. After two successful passages in the Australian wool trade, Moore was transferred back to the Tweed and Captain Richard Woodget, as a reward for his brilliant work on the Coldstream, was given command of the "Cutty" with very simple orders from John Willis: "Captain Woodget there is your ship. All you have to do is drive her."

Destiny was now about to take a hand.

VIII

"A WOODEN SHIP AND AN IRON MAN ROARING FROM NETHER HELL!"

> Roaring from Nether hell and filled with ice,
> Roaring and crashing on the jerking stage,
> An utter bridle given to utter vice,
> Limitless power mad with endless rage
> Withering the soul; a minute seemed an age.
>
> JOHN MASEFIELD, from *Dauber*

There exists in this world certain undefinable relationships that go beyond simple, logical explanations —
A boy for a dog, a woman for a man, a people for
a nation, a man for his ship, a ship for a man.

Woodget was the man — the Cutty Sark was the ship. Here was a man destined for greatness — here was a ship destined for immortality. Together their accomplishments have never been equaled. The driver pushed the driven; the driven tore at the bit, eager to perform, willing to burst her heart to please. This is the real story of the Cutty Sark!

To capture the mystique of the "Cutty," writers have quoted from her logs, sailing records, departure dates, dropping the names of mysterious Far Eastern ports of call — Whampoa, Foochow, Pagoda, Samarang, but they are all just words — sooner or later we must get to "The Heart of the Matter." Richard Woodget was a man wedded to a ship, and the Cutty Sark was every bit as much a part of his life as your family is to you. He teased, cajoled, petted, berated, and drove her. She responded to him. Between Woodget and the Cutty Sark a certain magic existed. He drove — she performed. She never disappointed him — he never failed her. She performed beyond expectation. She set records never to be surpassed in the annals of sailing history. Wood-

"The Salamis," from the painting by John Spurling.

get was the man — the Cutty Sark the ship, and like the thoroughbred she was, she responded to the master's touch like a thing of life.

Richard Woodget was born in 1845, the son of a Norfolk farmer, and at sixteen was apprenticed to the sea in a small British coastal trader the "Johns." For twenty years he served in practically every capacity on board ship: able body seaman, cook, steward and quartermaster, and mate, sailing to every corner of the world. From 1874 to 1880 he served as first mate on the "Copenhagen," seven hundred fifty-six tons, finally in 1881 winning command of John Willis' thirty-six year old "Coldstream." He drove the "Coldstream" fearlessly, making many excellent passages and consistently earning profits for Willis.

A total abstainer and non-smoker, he bore little resemblance to the typical master mariner of the day, and on shore he might have been mistaken for a local preacher. This, however, was never the impression

Courtesy National Maritime Museum

Captain Richard Woodget on board the Cutty Sark shortly before his death in 1928. The "Cutty" responded to his touch like a thing of life.

conveyed to a stevedore whom he caught carelessly stowing cargo in his ship.

He was a real "Captain Kettle" of the sea. He drove his ship and his men through all weather, and it is said that the Cutty Sark was never hove to while he was in command. But, he earned the respect of his men, oft times going aloft to inspect gear and rigging, condemning and having replaced anything worn or chaffed, and he never gave an order that he would not have been instantly ready to execute himself.

Woodget refused to spare himself in the service of his Cutty Sark. He would refuse to go below at sundown and would never leave an officer in charge as long as his ship was still under full sail. The old man would remain on deck for days at a time with little time off duty, watching the variations of the wind and clouds with eagle eye, ever ready to shorten sail whenever the occasion demanded.

Courtesy National Maritime Museum
The Cutty Sark in Sydney Harbour awaiting the wool clip. This photo was taken by Captain Woodget.

Woodget, besides being a magnificent shipmaster and driver, was quite an accomplished photographer, and considering the crude equipment available during those day, managed to take some most remarkable photos of the Cutty Sark during his ten years in command. In fact, almost all the surviving photos of the Cutty under sail are thanks to his efforts. On more than one occasion he had a boat lowered and with an apprentice or two rowing, set his box camera and tripod up and captured, on film, the Cutty Sark under full sail in mid-ocean.

The date is now April 1, 1885 — the time, 2:00 p.m. — the place, East India Dock — the ship, the Cutty Sark, and the test of her greatness is at hand. At sixteen, she is old by the "standards" of the times, starting a new life at sea, a new vocation, in a trade for which she was never intended, sailing oceans and weather and seas for which she was never designed. And yet, during her final ten years as a British clipper she will set records that will never be beaten or even approached by any other ship that will ever again sail the seven seas.

After departing the London Docks, Woodget arrived in Start Bay on his first passage to Australia, as master, on April 3. Not alone, the Cutty Sark was in the company of some of the largest, fastest and most modern iron wool clippers in the fleet, including the Samuel Plimsoll, Pengwern, Tythonus, and the River Fallock. To those who really knew their ships, the little tea clipper was no match for these powerful, driving, bohemoths. It was only a question of how badly she would be beaten. But let's see what happened. The "Cutty" covered the distance from the Start to the Equator in twenty-six days, made the Cape of Good Hope meridian twenty days later, dove down into the "Roaring Forties" and in her element, really clipped off the miles:

> May 21 — Lat. 45°15'S. Distance 316
> May 22 — Lat. 45°36'S. Distance 307
> May 23 — Lat. 46°05'S. Distance 308

This was followed by several more noon to noon runs approaching or exceeding three hundred miles per day. The "has been" showed the stuff she was made of, dropping her hook at Port Jackson, June 19, 1885, seventy-seven days from the Start. She beat the Samuel Plimsoll by one day, Pengwern by eight, River Fallock by fifteen and the Tythonus by eighteen days.

Captain Woodget now had another challenge at hand, passage round the Cape, for the first time, in command of the Cutty Sark. After loading his wool cargo, four thousand four hundred sixty-five bales, at Circular

The Cutty Sark loading wool at Circular Quay, Sydney. The bales of wool ready for loading can be seen stacked on the quay.

Quay, he departed for London on October 16, "Round the Horn." But the skeptics were determined to have their day. Woodget, the Cutty Sark, and her crew were the butts of an endless stream of jocular derision and puns directed at "the little toy clipper."

Man and ship were to be truly tested, for on heading towards the terrible Cape, the graveyard of sailing ships for three hundred years, he is purported to have said to his first mate, Jerry Dimint, "Double check the hatches, Mister, for we will soon have weather that will try not only men's souls but our good ship likewise." He didn't have too long to wait for his prediction to come true. Quickly working his way into the 50s, with a complement of only nineteen men, the weather and the seas started to build till it was blowing a strong gale. Struck by a terrible squall, she broached, with a tremendous sea almost sweeping the deck clean. The upper main topsail and the fore topgallant were blown clean off the yards, the main topgallant and main royal were torn to shreds. The "Cutty" was shipping enormous quantities of water, the outer jib stay parted, and the ship was in danger of foundering. Momentarily she hung there, hovering on the verge of death. Never before nor ever again would the Cutty Sark come so close to the edge of doom. Finally, she righted herself, shuddering and shaking off the millions of tons of cascading, boiling, foaming ocean that threatened to press her to the bottom of the sea. It must have been a night of horror for every man aboard. Woodget still drove on to the Cape, making repairs, bending, reefing, and setting new sails as best he could while the gale gradually blew itself out. "On she thundered" and with enormous seas washing round the Horn, she made Staten Island twenty-three days out of Sydney, striking up the Atlantic she crossed the line, twenty days from the Cape, a record for a Cape Horn to Equator run that has never been equaled. From here on it was all down hill, running home to London.

Woodget picked up his pilot at the Downs on December 28, 1885, a truly remarkable maiden passage, Sydney to London in seventy-three days. The Cutty Sark had beaten them all — Salamis by eight days, Thermopylae by nine, Loch Vennacher by eleven, Samuel Plimsoll by eighteen and the Cimba by twenty-two days. John Willis was so elated at her brilliant passage that he had a gilded "Cutty Sark" presented to Woodget to be flown from the main truck, poignantly commenting over the enthusiastic din of crew and visitors, as the sark was being carried up the mast, "We'el done Cutty Sark."

Ecstatic over the wonderful 1885 round the world passage that Woodget had logged, John Willis felt that his "Cutty" could still be a contender for tea cargo. He was not a man to give up easily. So it was that on February 19, 1886, the Cutty Sark departed the London River with orders for Shanghai. Although another "Cutty"-Thermopylae race was unlikely, Willis felt that at least Woodget could set a new Shanghai to London record. But, it all turned out to be fancy, for upon arriving in Shanghai on June 24, Woodget found Hallowe'en and Leander, the only two ships left in the great tea fleet, already awaiting what little cargo there was. Woodget and his agents spent three and a half months in a vain attempt to get a tea cargo. But for all their efforts there was none to be had. Leander loaded the last tea of the season and left Foochow for London on September 17. In disgust and in ballast, the Cutty Sark, under new orders departed for Sydney. After some terribly violent weather south of the Macclesfields Shoals, where she lost almost

*Rounding the Horn in a summer
gale.*

all the sail she was carrying, she managed from there on, a relatively uneventful passage to Sydney, arriving December 5, 1886.

Because of the time wasted in China, Woodget was too late for a wool cargo for the March sales in London, and he also missed all the other rivals for the 1886 race. Salamis and Thermopylae had a very close race, leaving Australia together on October 24, 1886, with Salamis beating Thermopylae to London by two days, arriving on January 17, 1887.

Well, after a three month wait Woodget finally managed to load a cargo and headed round the Horn once more. Departing Sydney on the afternoon of March 26, 1887, she caught a fresh breeze off Sydney Head which filled all sails and started the Cutty Sark on what was to be a very rough homeward passage. "Very hard south gale and terrific squalls," "Wind with mountain sea," "Mainsail split after being hauled up" are typical entries in the Log between Auckland Island and the Horn. It wasn't too long after these log entries that she ran into icebergs and remained amongst them for a whole week. These silent floating islands, oft times shrouded in fog, are a sailor's nightmare. A gentle

Courtesy National Maritime Museum

The Samuel Plimsoll, crack wool clipper beaten by the "toy clipper," Cutty Sark.

nudge by one of these monsters is enough to stove in a ship's hull and send her to the bottom. "Passed eight icebergs during the night" runs one succinct log entry. There is no need to comment further. But, Woodget, with iron nerves, kept all the sail the "Cutty" could handle pressed to the yards, through gale, ice or whatever forces nature could flaunt in his face. His iron nerve and his confidence in his ship paid off voyage after voyage. This one was no exception. The Cutty Sark had once again broken all records and beaten all contenders, the final results being:

Ship	Departed	Arrived London	Days Out
Cutty Sark	Sydney March 26, 1886	June 25	72
Mermerus	Melbourne Dec. 10, 1886	Feb. 26	78
Sir Walter Raleigh	Melbourne Dec. 10, 1886	Feb. 28	80
Salamis	Melbourne Oct. 24, 1886	Jan. 17	85
Thermopylae	Sydney Oct. 24, 1886	Jan. 19	87
Patriarch	Sydney Oct. 24, 1886	Jan. 21	89

The Cutty Sark was off again to Australia on August 17, 1887 and while running her easting down in the roaring 40's during the night of October 22, before a fresh S.S.W. wind, a W.S.W. squall hit her. Before the mate could give orders to have the ship come to, the fore topgallant backstay parted taking with it the royal backstay; over went the fore topgallant mast taking with it the fore topmast head, the main topgallant mast and the main topmast head. Luckily the gale abated a bit and somehow the wreckage was salvaged, and minimal repairs were made. The Cutty Sark never stopped. In fact, a fresh gale quickly made up and with most of her upper masts, yards and rigging gone she still managed to clip off the miles:

Oct. 22 214 miles
Oct. 23 228 miles
Oct. 24 156 miles
Oct. 25 265 miles
Oct. 26 280 miles

The Cutty Sark arrived in Sydney on November 14, eighty-nine days out, not a record by any means but certainly remarkable time considering the condition of her masts and rigging.

Woodget made it a habit to take the Cutty Sark well south in her run to the Horn, and ice, as dangerous as it was, was quite a common

The Salamis.

experience. The homeward passage of 1878 was no exception. C. Fox Smith describes Woodget's apparent disregard for the dangers surrounding his little ship in the terrible waters of the 60th Parallel. "When the ship was passing through ice, Captain Woodget used to lean on the spanker boom with his chin on his folded arms and watch the bergs, and many a time he found himself stuck fast to the boom by the beard when the time came to move. Another favorite diversion of his was a novel form of sea hopscotch — namely, trying to smash up some of the small ice, or "growlers" with the "Cutty's" bow, but they always dodged away on one side or the other. Woodget himself confirms the state of affairs that the Cutty Sark often found herself in — quoting from his log he describes the Cutty Sark's situation on January 11, 1878:

"Lat. 62°41'S. Long. 148°05'W. S85°E. 180 miles. Very high Wly. breeze, smooth sea. Up to noon passed 100 large icebergs and a great number of small. Noon, icebergs in every direction. Counted 87 from aloft, large ones besides little

The Loch Vennacher.

ones. Last night, when passing between 2 large icebergs, the thermometer fell to 31° and mist formed on the spanker boom and rails."

After rounding the Horn, favorable winds eventually brought the Cutty Sark to the Channel, she took her pilot off Dungeness on the 8th of March, completing the Newcastle to London run in sixty-nine days. Again she beat all the well known contenders — and all by a wide margin. The Thyatira, who left five weeks before the Cutty Sark, came up under her stern while she was hove to waiting to pick up her pilot. Mermerus was beaten by thirty days and the crack wool clipper, Loch Garry, was beaten by fourteen days.

During the first three homeward wool passages, under command of Captain Woodget, the Cutty Sark set records that to this day still stand.

She left again on the 18th of May, 1888, arriving in Sydney August 5, making a good but uneventful passage of seventy-seven days.

Tragedy however was to stalk the Cutty Sark on this homeward passage. Perhaps to "screw in" a few extra bales of wool, Woodget loaded less ballast than he ordinarily allowed and as a consequence the ship proved to be quite difficult to handle. He could not carry his royals nor his upper staysail, and with all his efforts to balance her sail complement, she was still exceedingly tender and constantly heeling over on her beam end, with decks always full of water, washing clean over the hatches. The tragedy happened — as so many similar tragedies have happened in the history of sail — while the men were working the sheets and braces waist deep in water, slipping, sliding, half-drowned, on a bitter cold, dark, and stormy morning. Captain Woodget recorded in the ship's log the tragic event that occurred that morning as follows:

Oct. 31 — Lat. 46°37'S. Long. 162°E. Course S39°E. Distance 202 miles. Strong winds and high confused seas. At 3 a.m. after hauling taut the lee main brace and before the men left the lee side, the ship was struck by a sea, which caused her to lurch suddenly and fill up all the lee side of the deck. Cooke, an apprentice, was washed over-board, he held on to a rope but before anyone could reach him, he lost his hold and was no more seen. The ship being under topsails only and heavy cross sea and dark, nothing could be done to save him.

The victim, Cooke, was making his first voyage on the "Cutty" having come out of Willis' "Dharwar." He was a promising youngster, possessing the makings of a good seaman.

Perhaps the ship herself sensed what had happened because this was one of the very few times she was ever beaten on the homeward passage. She arrived at the London Docks on January 20, 1889, the Loch Vennachar beating her by two days and the Salamis by one.

In 1891 she made a fair homeward passage of ninety-three days encountering light air almost all the way and in 1891/92 she beat the entire wool fleet with a fine passage of eighty-five days.

Two more years of excellent but relatively uneventful passages brings us to August, 1892, when the Cutty Sark departed on the 12th, from the South West India Dock for Australia. There was one single incident on this outward passage of 1892 that perhaps tells more about the brilliant sailing ability of this twenty year old "Queen of the Seas" than all the statistical documentation all of her biographers can ever hope to compile.

The tale is her remarkable victory over the crack P&O Line mail steamer, "Brittania," considered, at that time, to be the fastest ship in the world. Let William Morley, one of the Cutty Sark's crew, tell the story in his own simple seaman's language.

> We had a quick run down channel after carrying away our mizzen topgallant sail and a quick run to the Cape before our dead horse was worked up, that means before our months advance was up, so we had some pretty tall sailing, and a little over 60 days from the Cape to Sydney Heads, we passed several steam on the passage out. One passed us and we spoke to him for him to report us when he arrived at his port, and away he went. The wind freshened and we passed him. The old Man spoke to him again but he would not answer us. I think he got (riled up) because we were beating him and we left him hull down before sun set, we also sighted the Britannia at Green Cape that is 73 miles from Sydney Heads, and also asked him to report us at Sydney Heads alls well, which he answered allright, away he went, we had a nice breeze off the land doing about 12 knots. The wind freshened and we overhauled him and arrived into Sydney half an hour before he did. The Skipper asked the Pilot when he arrived at Sydney, where the "Cutty Sark" was, and he said there she is lying at anchor and the crew

CUTTY SARK IN SYDNEY HARBOUR. AUGUST 1891. CAPTAIN WOODGATE.

The Cutty Sark in Sydney, drying sails, August 1891.

coming down from up aloft after making the sails fast, and
the Master of the "Britannia" put it in the Sydney Bulletin;
(The Captain of the Cutty Sark asked me at Green Cape
to report him a Sydney Heads all well and he arrived a half
hour before I did).

The Cutty Sark loaded a cargo of wool for Antwerp and was at
sea on January 7, 1892. Again, it wasn't too long before she was in
the fog-bound ice fields of the 60th Parallel with two shivering deck
hands always on the lookout, ever attentive between the mournful blasts
of the foghorn, listening for the answering echo which would give
warning of the drifting death. And drifting death they certainly encoun-
tered. Again, Morley describes the scene.

We ran our Eastern down in 63° South of the Line, we
came amongst Ice Bergs and one, you may think it a tall

order, but I am not exaggerating we passed a Berg 1000 ft. high and 30 miles long not counting the small ones 2 or 3 miles long as well as small ice, we had 2 hands on the look out and the weather hazey and doing about 6 miles an hour so that is how he knew the big Berg was 30 miles long. 5 hours before we passed it. The fog lifted and when the old man saw what we had come through the old man was astounded to see what we had passed, we were all not sorry to leave the blighters behind.

Captain Woodget in the ship's log further tells of the terrors in the ice fields:

Found ice ahead, in fact, there was ice all round — as soon as we cleared one berg another would be reported on either side. You could hear the sea roaring on them and through them, the ice cracking sometimes like thunder, at other times like cannon, and often like a sharp rifle report, and yet could not see them.

At 1 p.m. the top of an iceberg was seen, which one could hardly believe was ice, it looked like a streak of dark cloud. Then we could see the ice a few feet down, but we could not see the bottom. It was up at an angle of 45 degrees, we were only about 1,000 feet off, so it would be 1,000 feet high. It had a circular top, but we could not see the ends. A few minutes later another was under the bows, we only cleared it by a few feet. It was about 100 feet high and flat-topped. Just as we were passing the corner there was a sharp report that made you jump, as if it was breaking in two.

Found another on the other side quite close, and a few minutes later saw the long ridge of ice almost ahead. Kept off, and then another came in sight on the other bow. We were too near it to keep away, but I felt sure it was no part of the big one — as we were passing this the point of the big one came in sight, the fog cleared and we passed in between them, there being not more than 400 feet between them.

When we had cleared the big one I saw its north end and took bearings. After sailing eight miles I took other bearings and found that the east side was nineteen miles long, and we could not see the end of the side we sailed along.

Icebergs, the drifting death, photographed by Captain Woodget, in 63° South Latitude.

We sailed about six miles alongside of it, water now quite smooth. Before noon the water was quite lumpy from all ways. After we had cleared the passage by about three or four miles, it cleared up astern, and what a sight it was! Nothing but icebergs through the passage and on the south side of the passage (for the south berg was only about half a mile long north to south, same height as the big berg: I expect it had not long broken off). There was nothing but a sea of ice astern, and another large flat-topped iceberg, which as far as you could see extended like land. It must have been twenty miles long or more. After we were through there was nothing but small ice, from small pieces to bergs 100 feet long. There was also one about a mile long covered with what looked like pumice-stone or lumps of tallow. I did not see it till it was abeam or I should have gone close to it; there was ice on either side of it. Ice now cleared.

However the Cutty Sark's trials were not yet over. By April 2, 1893, she was in the Bay of Biscay and upon encountering heavy weather and a nasty cross sea, Captain Woodget ordered sails to be reduced, ordering that the royal be taken in and the outer jib be hauled down. As two of the crew were on the jib boom, hauling the jib down, the ship's fore end suddenly dipped and the two men, John Doyle and John Clifton, were washed off the boom into the sea. William Morley, again, gives an account of the tragedy in his own words.

The old man gave orders to haul the outer jib down, while the men were out making it fast, she gave a dive and put the flying jib boom under about 5 ft. and washed the two men off the flying jib boom end, while I was making the Royal fast she nearly slung me over the yard and I could see she was full up fore and aft and coming down I saw the watch below on deck in their pants with the life buoy. I said who is overboard. They said Doyle and Clifton. I asked the Mate to get the Life Boat out. The Old Man said whirl ship as there was too much sea on to stay her, so we had to whirl ship that meant taking a scope of about 3 miles to go back to see if we could see any of the two men. I was still mad at the Mate about the Life Boat. I was expecting him to start on me.

Woodget turned the ship back and waited for two hours but failed to find the two missing hands in the wild, raging sea. Captain Woodget, a hard but terribly sensitive man, closed his log entry of April 2, 1893 —

> Fancy, only a minute before they were on the boom laughing to see the sprays come over the bows and the others getting wet, whilst they were dry on the boom; but one more minute, and things were changed: poor fellows, they were struggling in the waves. Doyle could not swim, so he sank to rise no more. Oh, what a gloom it cast over the ship! Two young men gone to Eternity, and only a few minutes before they were in high spirits and the best of health. During the seven years that I have commanded the Cutty Sark I never knew her to put the boom under before.

The Cutty Sark made Antwerp on April 15, 1893, and after months of lingering, looking for cargo, finally departed for Sydney on August 1, making the outward passage in eighty days. Loading a wool cargo of five thousand ten bales she departed for London on Christmas Eve, arriving in Hull on March 27.

She again departed for Australia, leaving East India Dock on June 25, 1894, for the last time under the red bunting. Although she was twenty-five years old, the Cutty Sark still consistently beat all modern ships who dared challenge her. In fact, some of the fastest times she ever logged were recorded on her last two voyages as a British clipper. On her 1893 outward passage she sailed five thousand nineteen miles in twenty days, averaging better than two hundred fifty miles a day, and on her final passage to Australia, she averaged two hundred thirty-three miles a day for thirty days. Still, she was not making money for John Willis. Her limited cargo capacity, her constant need of continuing repairs, her age were too much for him. On her arrival in London after the 1895 passage, he sold her, for two thousand one hundred pounds, to Messrs. J. A. Ferreira of Lisbon and she was renamed Ferreira.

IX
RELEGATED TO OBSCURITY

Beauty in desolation was her pride,
Her crowned array a glory that had been;
She faltered tow'rds us like a swan that died,
But although ruined she was still a queen.
JOHN MASEFIELD,
from "The Wanderer"

Life's battle is a continuing struggle where only the strong survive. To have seen this ragged, dishevelled ship it would have been hard to imagine that there was in her the strength of spirit to survive. But, strength grows stronger by being tried, and the old Cutty Sark had been dearly tried. The storm tossings which the sea had given her, made her the captain of her own soul. To look upon a ship as having a soul, drawing strength from it, of some enduring substance, not just a passing shadow in the night; to consider that she will shine forever and brighten a bit of eternity, carries with it something wonderfully agreeable to me.

Poor old-timer, soon to be forgotten by all, she would sail the seas for twenty-seven more years as "Ferreira." But within these wooden walls, like a being alive, there still breathed the barely perceptible pulse beat of immortality. Here was a ship who would refuse to die; humbled indeed, "relegated to obscurity," but with spirit unbroken.

Fondly called, by her Portuguese crew, El Pequina Camisola, she was to settle down to a life of obscurity as a trader trading between Tagus and the Portuguese colonies. For several years she made regular runs between Lisbon, Rio, New Orleans, and Oporto, carrying cargoes of coal, bricks, sugar, and lumber. From time to time we hear bits of news. Her owners wrote in 1909 "Ferreira" arrived today in Liverpool — fifty-nine days from Massomedes, "West Coast of Africa." They added: "This fast vessel has made, in our hands, several voyages and

The Ferreira, ex-Cutty Sark,
off Mossamedes.

we can give you the following: Lisbon to St. Paul deLoanda thirty-one days, Lisbon to Delagoa Bay fifty-three days and a record passage of twenty-nine days from New Orleans to Lisbon."

An officer in the Mercantile Marine saw the Cutty Sark in New Orleans in May of 1913 and sent this very moving description of her to Basil Lubbock who included it in his marvelous book *The China Clippers*:

Strolling leisurely one day along the water front at New Orleans, I noticed standing prominently out behind an old shed the tall tapering spars of a sailing ship. This class of cargo carrier being more the exception than the rule at the wharves of the Cresent city, and taking as I do a keen interest in the doings of the old clippers, my curiosity tempted me to investigate, so retracing my steps I made the best of my way

through a timber yard and eventually emerged upon the old
and dilapidated wharf at which she lay. The day of clipper
ships was past and gone long ere I commenced my apprenticeship in a modern Clyde four-poster, but I needed no
telling that this was one of the old timers.

The sun, high in the heavens, shone down with a dazzling
glare on her weather-beaten hull, painfully emphasizing
every detail of its shabby exterior and general air of neglect,
but though shorn of much of her former glory the unmistakable stamp of an aristocrat of the sea was ineradicable. It
shone forth despite her tattered gear and pitted bulwarks.
Like the old racer one sometimes sees relegated to the
'shafts,' the breed was unmistakable.

Floating lazily aloft with the shield and crown of
Braganza's noble house graven upon it, was the ensign of

Courtesy National Maritime Museum
The Ferreira at Surrey Docks.

Portugal. Wondering vaguely what old clipper she might be, I sauntered along the wharf admiring her graceful lines. She was ship-rigged with single topgallant sails and composite built. Her copper sheathing was visible apparently intact. Looking at her from forward, her entrance was like the thin edge of a wedge and it filled out gradually to her waist. A little fuller perhaps in the run, she had a handsome stern, whilst blazoned on her deep counter in 6-inch yellow letters was the legend "Ferreira Lisboa."

For a figure-head she had a comely maiden with swelling bosom and hand outstretched pointing ahead — plentifully bedaubed with multi-coloured paint. Though in hopes of finding some trace of her old name on the bows, I searched in vain — everything was obliterated and only the glaring "Ferreira" remained.

Making up my mind to go aboard, I glanced round to see if there was anyone in authority, whose permission ought to be asked. Everybody in the vicinity seemed to be enjoying their siesta. Several huge piles of staves (her cargo) lay around, upon which sundry 'niggahs' lazily basked, whiling the sunny hours as only a Southern nigger can. Walking over the gangway, I made my way slowly aft and mounted the poop.

To give the dagoes credit, they certainly did devote a little attention to this part of the ship though occasional startling splashes of colour (so dear to the Portuguese) struck a jarring note. The upper poop consisted of a raised deckhouse, some three and a half feet high. It was neatly railed and hammock-netted round. Along the port and starboard sides ran a row of garden seats. I call them garden seats as they were of a pattern more generally found in parks and gardens than on board ship. Two individuals occupied this poop, one worked away, stitching on the gore of a topsail, the other slumbered peacefully on one of the garden seats. The running gear all came down to the outer or lower poop, from which the mizen rigging was set up. Walking round this outer poop I came to the after end of the upper one, abaft which was the steering gear.

I examined the wheel and gear with interest, and also the brass bell, but though both were of an old pattern, I failed to find any trace of the ship's original name on either. Advancing on the individual who was goring the topsail and who, by the way, did not seem in the least disturbed at my presence, I addressed him —

"You speak English?"

He looked up and shook his head.

"Are you an officer?" I hazarded.

"No, sabe."

"Where is the captain?" I asked at last as a sort of forlorn hope.

The reply somewhat astonished me.

"Me capitan," he said, and went on with his work. I then made various gestures to signify I would like to see down below. He nodded acquiescence, so leaving him to his stitching and the "una pelota" (for such I took him to be) to his slumbers, I descended the after companion.

An alleyway led into the saloon on either side of which were doors with cut glass handles. The saloon was a fairly spacious apartment running athwartship. It was panelled neatly in teak and birds' eye maple and was adorned with much fancy carving. Beautiful as it had evidently once been, it was pretty bare now, the marble-topped sideboard and fireplace and the old brass lamp which swung in the skylight being probably the only original furniture left.

Another alleyway led from the saloon forward, and as I passed along it I glanced in through an open door into the captain's room. Like the saloon it was stripped of most of its old fittings, only a marble-topped washstand and a heavy, teak fourpost bed (the latter not often seen in ships nowadays) remaining. Various rooms occupied either side of the alleyway and at the end another companionway gave egress to the lower poop. Not caring to intrude I investigated no more of the rooms beyond noticing over the doors that old familiar legend "certified to accommodate one seaman."

Entering a door under the companion stairway I presently found myself in the after 'tween deck. Overhead the rust clung in huge scales to the diagonal tieplates and beams. The frames by the feel of them were still in a fair state of preservation, though they had not known a hammer or slice or paint for many a day.

Along the port and starboard sides ran a row of ports (now all plugged up) showing that at one time she had carried human freight here — emigrants, no doubt.

Coming to the main hatchway, I peered closely at its pitted surface endeavouring to decipher some letters and figures cut on the after coaming, but only managed to make out 63556 and 921100 tons.

Continuing forward through the fore 'tween decks which contained the usual miscellaneous collection of old junk, blocks and rusty wire, I came to the fore hatch. And as I looked down below at her wedgelike entrance, I thought that assuredly it needed clipper freights to make the ship pay. One could hardly find room to stand up on either side of the keelson, so fine was she. The iron collision bulkhead came down triangle-shaped, the apex at the keelson, and I mentally compared it with those of some modern windjammers and tramps which form nearly a square.

Retracing my steps aft and climbing through the after hatchway, I reached the deck again and was not sorry to feel the bright sunshine, for the old 'tween deck had a chilly, eerie atmosphere about it.

Gazing round, I now found many things to interest me. Her decks were badly rutted and cracked and sorely needed oil. Her rigging, fitted with wire lanyards (a doubtful boon) would have been better for a little tar and service. As the Yanks would say, they were "Hell on chains," chain strops being in abundance. And where a backstay had parted or a fore and after gone in the nip, the deficiency was supplied in this manner. A very handy device caught my eye abaft the main rigging, viz., a single winch barrel with double purchase and handle clamped to the topgallant pin rail. Apparently it could be used with equal facility for taking in a bit on the main sheet or bousing down the crossjack tack in a stiff breeze. It did not look, though, as if it had had much use of late.

The teakwood stanchions at the break of the poop, once a mass of shining brass and glistening varnish were now — ye gods! — painted with aluminum paint. It would have made an old deep-water mate grind his teeth to see such a desecration of the time-honoured methods of preserving "bright work."

Nearby a row of teakwood buckets stood in racks. These were brown painted and adorned with silver bands — too much trouble to scrub them, I suppose.

As I walked past I could not help glancing in to what had once been the half-deck. The door was open, so seeing no one at home I stepped in. A roomy enough place, it apparently once provided accommodation for quite a number of apprentices. It was now the abode of the petty officers; its old deal table, well-worn floor and battered bunks quite reminded me of old times. In the fore part of the after house a donkey room was situated containing an engine and winch of ancient pattern. Overhead were the boat skids upon which two launches and two boats rested in chocks, whilst on the deck above the old harness casks were still in possession.

The main fife-rail, inside of which the original old bilge pumps stood, was in pretty bad shape, though it must at one time have looked very fine with all its brass and carving. 'Way up above the rail I noticed the lower block of the topsail halliards, a chain pennant reached from it to the deck, a rope-saving device no doubt. The forward house, a neatly panelled structure, was identical with the half-deck but somewhat larger. She was well provided with boats, two more being on the top of this house — a wise precaution, as some day, like the "one horse shay" he will go to pieces all at once.

Making my way up the ladder, I reached the foc's'le-head, a pretty bare spot, enclosed by sundry rust-eaten stanchions with a ridge rope rove through them. Two pairs of hardwood bollards were placed on each side, on one of which a solitary brass cap glistened forlornly. The old whisker-booms were still in use, one out, the other in, all askew. The jib boom was rigged in, and as I looked at the old spar the lines of a deep-water song came to my mind.

"There was no talk of shortening sail by him who trod the poop,
And her boom with the weight of a mighty jib bent like a wooden hoop."

Looking over the side I again admired her clean entrance and knife-like bows. The old wooden-stocked anchors hung at the cat-heads, and the ring stoppers were fitted with a patent "tumbler" releasing gear eliminating the use of the time-honoured maul.

Coming down from the foc's'le-head, I had almost made up my mind to go when something caught my eye, which I had overlooked. Standing in pathetic solitude, suspended from a solitary cast-iron dolphin, was the old forward bell. Surely this would give me a clue to her name, I thought. I went up and examined it closely. Its surface appeared at first sight perfectly smooth, thickly coated with silver paint as it was. Presently, however, I thought I could discern a very faint trace of lettering. At which I extracted my knife and scraping away gently, gradually revealed the date 1869. I now hesitated, not caring to further mutilate the Portuguese artistic work, but reflecting that I might as well be hung for a sheep as a lamb, I took up my knife again. A few more strokes of the sharp blade and there, standing out boldly was a name, once a byword amongst seafarers, which raised a thrill such as that of the MAURETANIA or LUSITANIA could never raise — the CUTTY SARK! I tapped the old bell gently with my knife and heard again the mellow sound which through the trades, the tropics and the roaring forties had for nigh half a century marked alike the dark and the sunny hours.

Well, time was flying, and I had a long walk before me, so I made my way ashore. Standing on the wharf I surveyed her once more with a keener interest. The setting sun had almost reached the horizon. Its mellow, golden light, shining on her spars and rigging, seemed to transform her and clothe her in some of her ancient glory. Hidden were the marks of decay, and she once more looked the ship of speed and beauty.

More bits of news, here and there, reports in shipping papers and occasional notices of arrivals and departures help us track the Cutty Sark during her years of oblivion.

In June, 1915, Lloyds of London announced in its shipping news "Reported lost at sea, early this month, Ferreira ex Cutty Sark, bound from Lisbon to Mossamedes."

It's April 1916 and we hear of her shipping out of Delagoa Bay with a cargo of coal. The following month, she was totally dismasted in a cyclone, towed in to Table Bay — cut down and re-rigged as a barentine due to a shortage of materials and money. Again we hear of her in the London Evening News of October 22, 1921. "The Ferreira ex Cutty Sark arrived this date 50 days out of Pensacola, Florida, quite a remarkable voyage for a sailing ship over a half century old."

Lloyds Shipping Register in 1922 reported the sale of the Ferreira by Messrs. J. A. Ferreira & Son of Lisbon to Companhia Nacional ce Navegacao and renamed Maria do Anparo.

In September of 1922, almost unnoticed, still under her Portuguese name of Ferreira and caricature of a mere barkentine, the old Cutty Sark crept into Falmouth Harbor and dropped her hook, the last tack on a million mile voyage. Battered by a terrible Channel gale, desolation was rampant. She was in a filthy condition. The fragrance of the tea chests no longer clung about her hold, instead pigs slept in the fo'c'sle, a monkey was tied to the taffrail and dogs were sitting on deck mourn-

Courtesy National Maritime Museum

The Ferreira off Lisbon in 1915.

The Ferreira at Surrey docks. "Beauty in desolation was her pride."

fully scratching themselves. With her painted posts, rigging disarranged, yards ragged with tattered canvas, she was like a wounded sea-bird with a broken wing. Such was her condition when, on that eventful Fall day, Captain Wilfred Dorman, a retired ship master, saw this queen of the sea. "Beauty in desolation was her pride." Her spirit was untouched, she knew no sea that could tire her. Even in her degradation she carried the unmistakable air, the pose of the sea-bird come to rest upon the waves.

Captain Dorman saw through the dishevellment. Garish colors, painted posts, the strange barkentine rig could not hide her beautiful lines, her slim, graceful appearance. He recognized her as the Cutty Sark, the very same famous racer he so often saw and much admired while serving his apprenticeship at sea in the 1890s. Taeping, Sir Lancelot, Thermopylae — all had gone, all lying in fathomless, nameless graves, the currents swishing over their dead bleached bones. Only the Cutty Sark had survived. Captain Dorman saw her; she whom death could not daunt, as the true "Queen of the Sea" that she was — so stately and so still in such great peace. He was determined that he would someday see her stretching her fair canvas to the breeze, all shipshape and Bristol fashion with the Red Ensign once more flying from her peak.

X

"QUIET SLEEP — A SWEET DREAM" — "WE'EL DONE, CUTTY SARK"

> I must down to the seas again to the vagrant
>> gipsy life.
> To the gull's way and the whale's way where the
>> wind's like a whetted knife;
> And all I ask is a merry yarn from a laughing
>> fellow-rover
> And a quiet sleep and a sweet dream when the
>> long trick's over.
>> JOHN MASEFIELD, from *Sea Fever*

A dignified end is rare for a horse or a ship. The most famous of them have immortality in men's conversations but their own last days are a course set through degrading and humble tasks, ending at the abbattoir or the ship-breaker's yard. Captain Dorman was determined that the Cutty Sark, the most talked-about clipper of her day, would not share this fate. He bought her for three thousand seven hundred fifty pounds sterling from her Portuguese owner and had her towed home from Lisbon to Falmouth by the tug Triton. He planned to restore her to her original ship's rig and moor her in Falmouth Harbor that men might give her the reverence that was due her. She was the last of the great white winged sisterhood who were queens of the sea before the days of steam. Old men of the day, who went to sea as boys, spoke in awe of the occasions when the ships they sailed in tried to challenge the Cutty Sark in a test of speed. Legend was mixed with facts, historical tradition mixed with myth, but one thing was certain, any sailor who had served on her were celebrities in every dock-side tavern up and down the coast.

Looking along her deck in the fading light of that cold fall afternoon Captain Dorman must have imagined her dilapidation veiled, her slender spars once more clothed with a great press of canvas up to the

Courtesy The British Museum

The general appearance of the Cutty Sark at the time she was purchased by Captain Dorman from her Portuguese owners.

sky-sail poles. A man of action he wasted no time tackling the work at hand.

At his own expense, and with precious little information available as to her original sail plan, rigging details, and deck layout, he did, in fact, manage to refit her as a fully rigged ship. He completed this Herculean task in 1924 and used her for training boys "in the ways of a ship" until his death in 1936. His widow presented the Cutty Sark along with a trust fund of five thousand pounds sterling for her maintenance to the Incorporated Thames Nautical Training College. She was thence towed to Greenhithe and moored next to H.M.S. Worcester, a ship of the line, where she was used as an additional training ship for future naval officers.

After World War II, when the Worcester was replaced by the much larger steel built training ship Exmouth, the Cutty Sark was no longer required for training. There weren't sufficient funds available to adequately refit her and continue her general maintenance, so she was offered to the National Maritime Museum. Poor old Cutty Sark still hadn't found her final resting place. The Museum, due to lack of funds,

The Cutty Sark today, in permanent dry dock at Greenwich, England. A fitting monument to the British tradition of the sea.

was unable to accept her. Mr. Frank G. G. Carr, one of the "Cutty's" most formidable mentors, and a man who like Woodget did not give up easily, approached the London County Council. Sir Isaac Hayward, Chairman of the Council, responded to the idea of making the Cutty Sark a historical monument with great enthusiasm. A great deal of money and research would be required to refurbish her to her original state and the London County Council felt it could not burden the tax payers with this expense. However, as an emergency stop-gap measure, the Council advanced the sum of four thousand pounds sterling for minimal repairs and repainting in order to make her presentable as an exhibition. She was then towed to Greenwich and moored in the river, in time to be seen by visitors during the Festival of Britain.

It was obvious to all that further steps had to be taken to protect the Cutty Sark and guarantee her permanent preservation. At this point in time His Royal Highness, The Duke of Edinburgh, became another active mentor. From his personal intervention grew the Cutty Sark Steering Committee, which quickly became the Cutty Sark Preservation Society under the Chairmanship of Mr. Henry Barraclough, M.V.O. The first goal of the Society was to raise, by public subscription, two hundred fifty thousand pounds sterling, which was the estimated sum to build a permanent dock for her in Greenwich, and to totally restore her for permanent public exhibition. On May 28, 1953, she was formally handed over to His Royal Highness, The Duke of Edinburgh, Patron of the Cutty Sark Preservation Society.

The British people responded in magnificent fashion, truly rising to the occasion. The land on which her dry dock was to be built was donated by the London County Council, Sir Robert McAlpine & Sons, Ltd. built the dock at cost, Messrs. R & H Green and Silley Weir, Ltd., agreed to restore and rerig her on a no profit basis. Messrs. Martin Black (wire ropes) Ltd. offered over two miles of wire standing rigging as a gift. All the terylene (dacron) fibre for the running rigging, enough in fact to make fifty thousand "wash and wear" shirts, was presented by Imperial Chemical Industries and made into rope free of charge as a gift by the Gourock Ropework Ltd. It went on and on: gifts of money, time and material came in from all over the Commonwealth. This was certainly another of Great Britain's "Finest Hours."

The dock was completed on December 10, 1954, and the Cutty Sark was moved to permanent berth by three tugs, again provided free by Messrs. William Watkins Ltd.

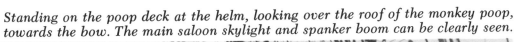

Standing on the poop deck at the helm, looking over the roof of the monkey poop, towards the bow. The main saloon skylight and spanker boom can be clearly seen.

The old "Jig'y Jig" windlass. The windlass itself is housed underneath the forecastle deck. The crossed poles are the windlass arms, and were unshipped and stowed in this fashion when not in use. The original ship's bell hangs off the Sampson post.

The hull was found to be in remarkably good condition when surveyed in the dock. In fact, abstracting from Mr. Frank G. G. Carr's most excellent technical paper, "The Restoration of the Cutty Sark," he reported the following.

She had 430 tons of sea sand ballast, not evenly spread but heaped up amidships, which had rotted the ceiling and fallen down between the floors, so that their condition could only be guessed. Yet when the water had left the dock and she was supported only on the keel blocks and shores, and Mr. Charles Maddox measured the "breakage" he found it to be no more than 5/16th of an inch. This compares with the ¼ inch found by Scott & Scantlebury in 1937. By any standard, it is an astonishing result.

The bottom of the ship had been lined with cement when she was built. What was really astonishing was the discovery that under the cement there was no trace of rust and the original red oxide paint was still intact on the frame. Remarkable also, the cement had nowhere been cracked, either by the working of hull or the pressure of corrosion. Most astonishing of all was that even in the bottom of the ship, where

The deck winch, besides being used for general cargo purposes, was also used to haul in the anchor chain. The chain was fed into the chain pipes on the deck to the chain locker below. The base of the foremast, the double main stays, and the fore fife rail can also be seen.

there was likely to have been salt bilge water sluicing around, the iron frames were quite unaffected where the bolts passed through them, making a snug fit with the nut hove up tight.

The main objective of The Cutty Sark Society was to restore her to her original condition as a crack tea clipper of the 1870s. But, this was not going to be an easy task. First, the firm who completed her after Scott & Linton went bankrupt had long since gone out of business, and the only known set of original plans had been lost in a fire in Glasgow shortly after the Second World War. Secondly, this eighty-five year old ship had undergone many undocumented changes by her captains and owners alike. The Society came to the stark realization that

The Cutty Sark's wheel and steering-gear box. All the gears and mechanisms related to turning the rudder are housed in this box whose lid is in two halves and hinged.

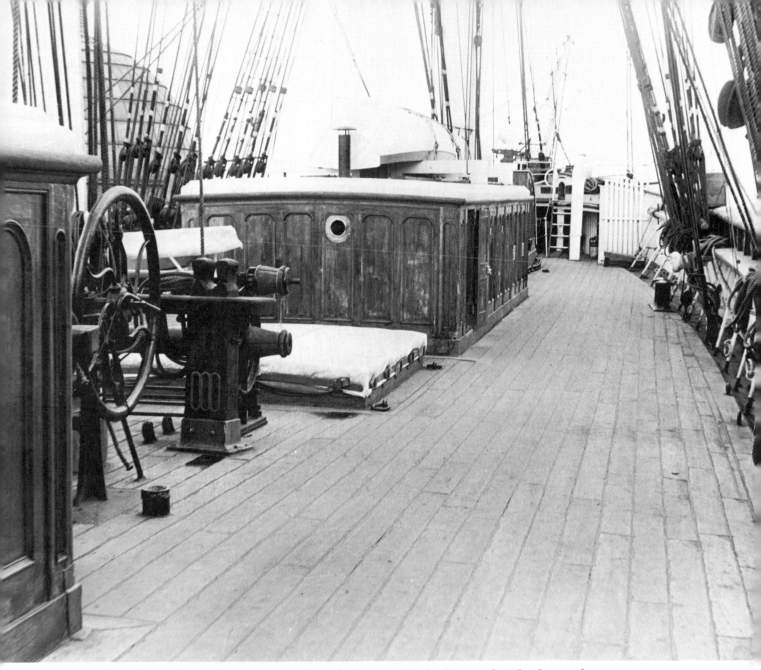

Looking down the starboard sweep of the deck towards the forecastle. The forward deck house housed the galley and quarters for twelve seamen.

they really didn't know what the Cutty Sark looked like in 1870. A tremendous research program, by all concerned, was instituted, and it paid off handsomely. Her original profile and plan, drawn by John Rennie, her chief draftsman, was found in the Glasgow Museum. This drawing was of inestimable value, showing her original deck plan as designed and laid out by Linton. Of particular interest was the fact that it showed that the "Cutty" originally had been designed with only a forward deck house. Further detective work located John Rennie's

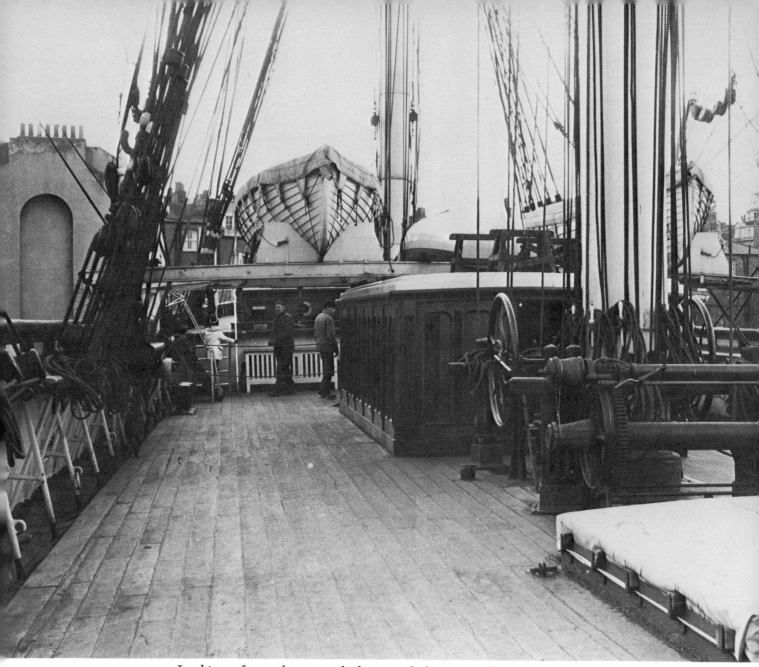

Looking aft up the main deck toward the poop. The main mast, thirty inches in diameter at its base, is nestled in between the main pumps and the cargo winch.

son in Mombassa who had in his possession his father's original drawing for the midship section.

The daughter of Henry Henderson, Master Shipwright of Scott & Linton and the "Cutty's" first carpenter, was located in Greenock. Here the search struck gold, for she had in her possession Henderson's original notebook in which he had recorded every dimension of every spar and mast on board. Also in her collection of memorabilia were two photos of Moodie's famous jury rig rudder. One of these also showed the general arrangement of the original beautiful carving and guilding around the stern, all of which had long since disappeared.

In December, 1955, the granddaughter of Hercules Linton came forth with John Rennie's original sail and rigging plan. By now almost all the pieces of the puzzle were fitting together. Finally, in a Montreal department store, the last major bit of detective work fell into place.

Some of the intricate wood carvings of the stern, including the long lost "Star of India." The star and rays are gold, the ribbon blue with gold lettering and edges, and the star itself sits on a red background.

In an accidental encounter Commander Alan Villiers, met a Mr. S. E. Appleton, who as a child played with David Kirkaldy-Willis, nephew of old "White Hat Willis." He knew of the whereabouts of David's widow. Here again was another wonderful find, for Mrs. Kirkaldy-Willis had in her possession the large carved and guilded "Star of India," the key piece necessary to complete the stern detail. She also had Willis' own painting of the Cutty Sark under full sail, rendered by F. Tugday in 1872. This painting showed the "Cutty" with an after deckhouse and confirmed that the after house had been built by 1872 and possibly even at the time of launching by Denney Bros. The painting also showed the deck houses had varnished teak panels, not painted white as most contemporaries thought. Most important, it also confirmed much of the rigging detail drawn by John Rennie.

Except for the gilded cutty sark that Willis had presented to Captain Woodget in 1885, and which was believed to have been lost at sea, the search was over.

The beautiful hand-carved scrollwork decoration of the stern. The scrollwork is all in relief, gold gilded on a black background.

The bow, showing the figurehead of Nannie, the witch, reaching out to grab Meg's tail. The very fine gilded scrollwork can also be readily seen.

Then a remarkable thing happened. But let Mr. Frank G. G. Carr tell it in his own words. It must have been a terribly exciting moment for him.

The last detail required to complete the restoration was the original "cutty sark" itself; the short chemise cut out of sheet metal and mounted eccentrically to act as a wind vane, which was shipped on a spindle on the truck of the main skysail pole when in port in order to distinguish the ship from her rivals. Captain R. J. Woodget had confirmed that this had been in the ship when she was sold to the Portuguese in 1895, but since that date nothing had been heard of it. At 10:30 a.m. on Thursday, November 10, 1960, a telephone call informed the author that what was believed to be this original emblem was coming up for auction as an early lot in a sale beginning at 11:00 a.m. that morning in a small auction room near Chancery Lane. Time did not allow inspection, but a chance was taken, bidding arranged, and the item bought. When collected, it was found that mounted in a frame with the "sark" itself was a certificate, signed and sealed by the Portuguese Consul at Capetown in 1916, to the effect that this was the original emblem rescued from the masthead when the ship had been dismasted, and presented by the Captain to Mr. F. de Q. de Gruchy, a private collector of Africana. Mr. de Gruchy had recently died, and on his death, among various of his effects sold in London had been this relic of the "Cutty Sark."

To add further proof of authenticity, a photograph was taken and sent to Captain R. J. Woodget at his home in Norfolk, and he immediately confirmed that this was the original "sark" that he, when senior apprentice, had so often carried aloft and shipped in place on arrival in port.

Again I must call on Mr. Frank Carr, who labored so diligently to restore our "Queen of the sea" to her pristine beauty, to describe her resting in her quiet sleep — her sweet dream.

In order to make all parts of the ship accessible to the public, and to enable visitors to gain some appreciation of what the clipper ship represented in the history of merchant sail, it was necessary to accept certain departures from a complete restoration to her 1870 condition. Greatly to be regretted was the necessity to retain, for ventilation purposes, the row of ports on both sides of the 'tween deck, inserted when she was being used as a training ship. The alternative, to provide an artificial ventilation system with trunking and the noise of fans would, however, have been even more objectionable. To provide an entrance on the level, a gangway bridge from the dock side leads into the 'tween deck through entrance doors cut through the side amidships. An escape route from the upper deck in case of fire is provided by a replica of the accommodation ladder on the starboard quarter, but made wider than the original, which is lowered in daytime to a bridge across to the dock side. It is hoisted up at night to avoid unauthorized entry. As an additional safeguard, an opening through the bottom amidships and alongside the centre line keelson, with a self-operating ladder lowering into the bottom of the dock, will shortly be constructed, whereby it will be possible to escape from the lower hold without passing through the 'tween deck. An extensive fire sprinkler system has been provided throughout. A complete new deck has been constructed in the lower hold, with a wooden bulwark surrounding it, and wide stairways leading down from the 'tween deck at both the forward and the after end. A central handrail divides

The saloon in the main cabin. This is the most spacious living area in the ship. It is panelled in teak and bird's-eye maple and generously adorned with fine wood carvings. It has a marble topped sideboard and fireplace and a fine brass lantern swings in the skylight.

descending from ascending traffic, a very necessary precaution when holiday crowds are on board. Similar wide stairways lead from the 'tween deck to the upper deck, where their exits are covered by hooded companion hatches

A view from the wheel showing the tremendous complexity of the standing and running rigging. There are over two miles of standing wire rigging alone.

A close-up view of the main top, showing some of the mast hardware, including the lower yard tress, related to trimming the lower main yard.

panelled in teak in the same style as the deckhouses, so as not to be too obtrusive. To give protected access to the cabin accommodation aft, it has also been necessary to retain the tall hooded companion hatch fitted by the Portuguese, instead of replacing it by the original low-built fitting. In the 'tween deck, necessary accommodation for the present officers and crew has been provided on either side, forward of the entry doors, hidden behind partitions which have been

Looking up the fore mast, showing the fore upper topsail yard (second from the bottom) with the stunsail booms in place.

covered with "mock-ups" to represent on the port side, chests of China tea as shipped in the eighteen-seventies, and on the starboard side, bales of wool as carried in the eighteen-eighties, when the Cutty Sark was an Australian wool clipper. Opposite the entrance doors is a counter for the sale of publications and souvenirs, and aft of this starts a series of screens running round both sides telling in pictorial form chronologi-

In my mind's eye, here was a ship. Take her for all in all, we shall not look upon her like again.

cally the story of "The Cutty Sark and the Days of Sail."
Show cases and screens in both the 'tween deck and the
lower hold are filled with exhibits, including original logs
and journals of the ship, the model of the Cutty Sark made
by the late Sir Maurice Denny, which is probably the finest
clipper ship model in the world, a recently acquired model
of the ship when Portuguese-owned and rigged as a barquen-
tine, sextants, chronometers and the like. To these have been
added objects from the remarkable and world-famous private
museum of the late Mr. John Sidney Cumbers, known as
"Long John Silver," once exhibited in his house at Gravesend, the whole of which he generously presented to the
Cutty Sark Society. Of outstanding interest from this source
are the fifty merchant ship figureheads exhibited in the lower
hold, representing just under half his collection, numbering
one hundred one in all, easily the largest and finest collection
of its kind in the world.

Today the Cutty Sark rises proudly in her Greenwich setting, a
monument to the great British tradition of the sea.
May I, in closing, slightly alter those famous words from Hamlet:

> In my mind's eye, here was a ship.
> Take her for all in all.
> We shall not look upon her like again.

APPENDIX

APPENDIX A

John Robert Charles Spurling
Marine Artist Extraordinary

Si talked with Dauber, standing by the side,
"Why did you come to sea, painter?" he said.
"I want to be a painter," he replied,
"And know the sea and ships from A to Z,
And paint great ships at sea before I'm dead;
Ships under skysails, running down the trade-
Ships and the sea; There's nothing finer made."
JOHN MASEFIELD, from "Dauber"

Putting ideas on canvas has brought fame to a number of artists. Their works run the gamut from pastorals to portraits covering virtually all of history's pictorial themes. Many of them attempted to portray the sea, few were successful. Their numbers are reduced even further when you classify them into the special realm of windship artists. Of those who tried capturing the living, bounding clippers on canvas, tried to show them in their elements — wild wind and roaring sea — few succeeded. The one who succeeded more than most was Jack Spurling — sailor, actor, bon vivant, world traveler, artist — the man who left a treasure trove of clipper ship paintings for posterity. This is his story in so far as The Compass has been able to piece it together from back issues of *The Blue Peter, Sail,* and from one of his sons, Denzil Spurling.

John Robert Charles Spurling, as he was christened, first saw the light of day on December 12, 1870. His parents, Charles and Mary McCallam Spurling, had a fairly large family — two sons and four daughters. His father was a prosperous importer dealing mainly in jute, a trade that gave Jack his first contact with the sea. This early, albeit distant, exposure to ships and the sea was destined to develop into a lasting romance that is magnificently expressed in his superb paintings.

From birth Jack was a delicate child. During his early years he developed a serious

---

This essay reprinted through the kind permission of Mr. K. V. W. Lawrence, editor of the Mobil Oil Corporation publication, *The Compass.*

kidney affliction, a disability that would plague him throughout his life. But this did not hamper him or interfere with his education, which included lessons in art and music. Though every member of the family had some artistic bent, it was Jack who showed real promise. His art teacher told his mother while Jack was still comparatively young that he could ". . . teach the budding young genius very little since he has progressed far beyond this teacher's ability."

As a schoolboy in the 1880s, he spent many of his free hours along London's docks. But let him tell his own story. Speaking to Mr. F. A. Hook, editor of *The Blue Peter*, he had this to say:

"My one pleasure as a boy was painting ships, and at the age of ten I was frequently at the East India Docks (Blackwall) drawing the beautiful vessels of such lines as the Aberdeen White Star, Shaw Savill, Devitt & Moore, Carmichael, A. L. Elder, Trinder, Anderson & Co., Anderson, Anderson & Co., James Duthie, Aitken Lilburn & Co., — owners of the famous Lochs — and John Willis & Son. In those days one could walk a mile along the quays under the ships' big bowsprits with jib booms all run in, their beautiful carved figureheads all leaning forward as if straining to be free from the chains and wire ropes that held them captive. Up the sides of these ships I used to climb, to wander round their decks, go into the boys' house, as the apprentices' berth was called, and, at times, have a yarn with the boatswain or ship-keeper — types of seamen one does not meet now, for they seem to have disappeared with the ships. I remember, particularly, one day aboard the Mermerus. She was sailing in a few days for Melbourne. The year, I believe, was 1885. I had been making sketches of the ship and was wandering about her decks watching the riggers at work finishing the bending of ropes and sails when a man came out of the cabin and asked me 'what the hell' I wanted. I said I wanted to see the men at work, as I intended to go to sea. He turned away and gave a laugh, a laugh I have never forgotten. Then he came up to me and said: 'A man who goes to sea for pleasure goes to hell for pastime. It's a dog's life, I tell you, boy! Keep away from ships, or as sure as God made little apples, they will get you,' and he walked into the cabin. The speaker was Captain Cole, the commander of the Mermerus.

"These ships had a fascination peculiar to themselves, a fascination one does not find now — the mixed odors of spices from the East, of tar and marling, hemp and coir, the music of the wind through their gear strung on great spars and masts — were to me irresistible."

In spite of Captain Cole's warning, the "irresistible" lure of ships caused Jack Spurling to ship out on the Astoria when he was only sixteen. The ship, built in America and commanded by Captain G. Jackson, was on her first voyage out from England under the red duster. Her destination was Singapore with a cargo of coal. She was known as an unlucky ship and proved to be especially so for Jack Spurling. While working sail off Anger Point (Sumatra), he fell from the main upper topsail yard to the deck suffering injuries that were to confine him to a Singapore hospital bed for five and a half months. Fortunately for him, he landed on a coil of rope, a factor that probably saved his life.

Recovered, he returned to London aboard the S/S Glenorchy. Once again he met with an accident that nearly cost him his life. While the ship was anchored in Bitter

Lake, probably awaiting the southbound convoy, he was away in one of her small boats. The boat capsized nearly drowning him. Fortunately, fate again took a hand; all he got was wet and scared.

Back in London he entered the services of Messrs. Devitt & Moore. After serving the regulation period in sail, he obtained his second mate's certificate and joined the Blue Anchor Line as a junior officer. He had this to say about his seagoing career:

"At sea I had the opportunity of studying under all conditions the beautiful ships I had known as a boy. I think I can safely say that if I once ran my eye over a ship that took my fancy, I never forgot her lines, nor little of her detail; a ship and her spars were always something very near my own heart, and it was with a pang that as a full-time apprentice I said good-bye to the masts and yards one foggy day at the London Dock."

When he was just eighteen years old and still serving at sea as a midshipman, a notice appeared in the March 29, 1889 issue of *Fairplay*. This was a real push along the road to fame and brought him to the attention of the shipping fraternity. It read:

"A new marine painter has come about in the person of Mr. J. R. C. Spurling. This gentlemen, who is very young, has been to sea all his life, but having a remarkable talent for painting vessels and putting them in a sea that looks like a sea, he has now given himself up to the work. Two of his water colours, the OROYA(S) and the AUGUSTA VICTORIA(S) are about the best things of the kind I have seen. His address is 27 Leadenhall Street, and I advise anyone wanting a steamer well drawn to apply to him."

Spurling stayed at sea for roughly seven years. About his coming ashore and subsequent career, this is what he told Mr. Hook:

"After leaving the sea, I practised, in and out and turn about, marine painting, and the dramatic art. Under the management of the late George Edwardes I played leading parts in *A Runaway Girl, The Messenger Boy, Toreador, Geisha*, and many other plays. Later I was engaged by Mr. Robert Courtneidge to play the Indian Prince in *The Blue Moon*, my favourite part. My stage career took me to sea again, for I visited India, Australia, and New Zealand. Then came an engagement to play at Daly's theatre with Mr. Robert Evett's Company, in *The Maid of the Mountains* and *A Southern Main*. Here, on several occasions, it fell to my lot to play the lead, for Mr. Bertram Wallis, with Miss Jose Collins — a great pleasure, needless to say. Throughout my connection with the stage I continued to paint ships, mostly commissioned by their owners. At last, despite tempting offers to remain on the London stage, the demands on my brush compelled me to give up the theatre and to devote my whole time to painting."

Jack Spurling's superb touch came to F. A. Hook's attention when the latter was the Public Relations Officer of the Peninsula & Oriental Steam Navigation Company (P & O) and editor of its house magazine, *The Blue Peter*. Hook, who recognized Spurling's talents, knew the artist could be of considerable service to the magazine. He purchased all the then available Spurling paintings and commissioned him to do a series of clipper ship studies to be used on the magazine's covers. The first one appeared in the March, 1923, issue, and the series was a big feature until the artist died. As a matter of record, the work was so well done that *The Blue Peter* offered a reward (one thousand pounds sterling) to anyone who could find a mistake in the sails, the running or standing rigging. As far as we know, the reward was never paid. Anyone who is fortunate enough to see one of the originals can readily see why.

The Blue Peter was responsible for spreading his name and his fame to the ends of the earth. It brought him inquiries from many former shipmates. Many of them who saw the paintings, though they would comment critically on the work, did so with a feeling of pride. They were delighted with his record of ships, and sailors of a rapidly passing era were proud to have known him. One old salt even wrote in to find out if the artist was "the same chap Spurling who used to daub in oils on old sailcloth."

The paintings he did for *The Blue Peter* were done mainly from drawings and plans he obtained from various shipping companies. His genius was the ability to translate them into living, breathing ships in all situations from at anchor to running down their eastings in the roaring forties. As one critic wrote of him after his death, "He was sometimes criticized for his imagery, but, as an old sailing man myself, I think the gods must have sent him as a balm for the mortification which old sailors felt at the disappearance of the clipper ship." What finer testimony could one ask than that. You have only to look at one of Jack Spurling's magnificent paintings to see that it's a testimony well earned.

The Compass learned that many of the paintings were done in the unbelievable time of two or three days. He was always optimistic, never worried about tomorrow. Actually we are inclined to believe that he painted only to keep the wolf from the door. According to his son Denzil, he was a fiery, colorful character, always the temperamental artist.

The bad health and kidney trouble that periodically bothered him took over in 1931. For two years his production was relatively nil as his sickness grew more and more pronounced. Finally, after a very serious operation, he sailed on his last voyage to beyond the far horizon. The date was May 31, 1933 and the place, Seamen's Hospital, Greenwich. The cause of death was given as Empyema and Renal Calculus.

Since his death, Jack Spurling's paintings have followed the art world's trend and have grown in value. An exhibit of his works held in 1939 elicited this review from London's *The Times*:

"At the Stevens and Brown Gallery, 8, Seamore Place, Park Lane, there is the first public exhibition of 34 water-color drawings and a few oil paintings of famous sailing ships, by the late Mr. Jack Spurling, who after following the sea and the stage, died in 1933 at the age of 62. The 'Astoria,' in which he made his first voyage at the age of 16, is included in the exhibition. Naturally, the pictures will appeal chiefly to those who have associations with the ships, but while they have the technical accuracy of the expert seaman, they also show a fine sense of weather and movement. One of the oil paintings shows the famous race, in 1872, between 'Thermopylae' and 'Cutty Sark,' and among the water-colors 'Cedric the Saxon' and 'Sobraon' may be specially noted. The catalogue has notes on the ships and their histories."

When Mr. Hook died, his widow, not knowing the value of the paintings, sold them at public auction. Most of them disappeared into private collections, some even finding their way to the United States. The editor, with the help of two Spurling enthusiasts, Mr. Rex Vivian (owner of the "Salamis") and Mr. Warren Moore (owner of the "Loch Etive"), has uncovered nine others: "Ariel," "Sophocles," "Patriarch," "Middlesex,"

"Miltiades," "Waimate," "Taranaki," "Thomas Stevens" and "Duntrune." We have learned also that a Spurling original, "The Hesperus," was recently lost in a Los Angeles fire. The possibility exists that several others have been lost, particularly during World War II. But by and large a fair majority of them can be found in private collections.

APPENDIX B

The Caliph's outfit, typical of all A-1 Lloyds registered clipper ships as taken from the original builders contract.

CHAINS AND ANCHORS

	Cwt.	Qrs.	
2 bowers,	27	3	Brown Lennox make.
1 bower,	25	1	Trotman's patent.
1 stream,	11	0	
1 kedge,	5	25	
1 kedge,	2	3	

With 300 fathoms of 1 11/16 chain, and 60 fathoms of 15/16 mooring chain. 6 boats, each 26 feet long; 2 lifeboats, 1 gig, and 1 cutter.

STANDING RIGGING

WIRE RIGGING

Size

Fore main rigging and stays	5 ins.
Mizen rigging and stay	4 ins.
Fore and main topmasts, backstays, and stays	4¾ ins.
Mizen main topmast, back stays, and stays	4 ins.
Fore and main topgallant backstays	3 ins.
Fore topgallant and flying jib-stays	3 ins.
Main topgallant stays	3¼ ins.
Mizen topgallant stay and backstay	2¾ ins.
Fore and main royal backstay	3 ins.
Fore royal stay	2¾ ins.
Main royal stay	2½ ins.
Mizen royal backstays	2¾ ins.
Mizen royal stay	2¼ ins.
Fore and main skysail backstay	2 ins.

Fore and main skysail stays .... 1¾ ins.
Mizen skysail stays .... 1½ ins.
Mizen backstay .... 1¾ ins.
Outer and inner jib-stays .... 3¾ ins.
Outer and inner jib-boom guys .... 3½ ins.
Flying jib-boom guys .... 3¼ ins.
Fish and cargo pendant .... 4½ ins.
Fore and main topmast rigging...................................... 2¾ ins.
Mizen and main topmast rigging .... 2½ ins.
Fore and main topgallant rigging .... 2 ins.
Man ropes for bowsprit .... 2¼ ins.
Mizen topgallant rigging .... 2 ins.
Main brace pendant.. 4 ins.

FOOT ROPES (FOUR-STRAND CORDAGE)

Fore and main foot ropes .... 3½ ins.
Crossjack, lower, upper fore and main topsail ropes .... 3¼ ins.
Mizen topsail, fore and main topgallant foot ropes .... 3 ins.
Mizen topgallant foot ropes .... 2¾ ins.
Fore and main royal foot ropes .... 2½ ins.
Mizen royal foot ropes .... 2¼ ins.
Fore, main and mizen skysail foot ropes .... 2 ins.
Standing boom foot ropes .... 3½ ins.
Flying boom foot ropes .... 2 ins.

RUNNING RIGGING

RUNNING GEAR

Main topmast and staysail halds. 2¾ in., downhauls .... 2¼ ins.
Main topgallant and staysail halds. 2¾ in., whip 2 in., downhaul ..... 2 ins.
Main royal staysail halds. 2¼ in., downhaul .... 24 thds.
Mizen topmast staysail halds. 3 in., whip 2 in., downhaul .... 2 ins.
Mizen topgallant staysail halds. 2¼ in., downhaul .... 24 thds.
Mizen royal staysail halds. 2 in., downhaul......................... 21 thds.

SPANKER GEAR

Head outhaul whip and downhaul 2¼ in., tripping line .... 2 ins.
Foot outhaul 3 in., lower and upper brails .... 2 ins.
Gaff topsail sheet 2¾ in., halds. 2½ in., downhaul .... 2 ins.
Gaff topsail tack 2¾ in., tripping 24 thds., brail .... 24 thds.
Jamie Green halyards 2¾ in., sheets 2½, tack 2½, tripping line ...... 2 ins.
Crossjack sheets 3 in., crossjack life .... 2¾ ins.
Fore and main lift falls .... 2¾ ins.

Boats' tackle falls .... 2¾ ins.
Ring tail halds. 3¼ in., whip 2¼ in., sheet 2¾ in., tack 3 in., main bowline 3 in.
Fore and main clew-garnets .... 3¼ ins.
Fore and main reef-tackles .... 2¾ ins.
Fore and main buntlines 2½ in., whips .... 2¼ ins.
Fore and main leechlines .... 2¼ ins.
Fore and main topsail clewlines .... 2¾ ins.
Fore and main reef-tackles .... 2½ ins.
Fore and main topsail buntlines .... 2½ ins.
Fore and main topgallant clewlines .... 2½ ins.
Fore and main topgallant buntlines .... 2¼ ins.
Fore and main royal clewlines .... 2¼ ins.
Fore and main royal buntlines .... 24 thds.
Fore and main skysail clewlines .... 21 thds.
Fore and main skysail buntlines .... 21 thds.
Fore bowlines .... 3¼ thds.

STUDDING-SAIL GEAR

Lower studding-sail hyds. 3½ in., whip 2½ in., downhaul 2¼ in.,
    sheet .... 3½ ins.
Lower studding inner do. 3 in., tack .... 2¾ ins.
Lower studding-sail boom topping-lift 5 in., whip .... 2½ ins.
Lower studding-sail guy 5 in., whip 2¾, foreguys .... 3 ins.
Fore and main topmast studding-sail hyds. 3½ in., whips .... 2½ ins.
Fore and main topmast studding-sail tack 3 in., sheet 3½ in.,
    downhaul .... 2¼ ins.
Fore and main topmast studding-sail boombrace 4 in.,
    whip 2¾in., top. lift .... 3 ins.
Fore and main topgallant studding-sail sheet 2¾ in., downhaul .... 2 ins.
Fore and main topgallant studding-sail hyds. 2¾ in., tack .... 2½ ins.
Fore and main royal studding-sail hyds. 2¼ in., tack 2 in.,
    sheet 2¼ in., downhaul .... 24 thds.
Fore skysail studding-sail hyds. 2 in., tack 24 thds., sheet .... 2 thds.
Crossjack bowline 2½ in., clew garnets 2¾ in., buntlines 2¼,
    leechlines .... 2 ins.
Mizen topsail clewlines 2¼ in., reef tackle 2¼ in., buntlines .... 2½ ins.
Mizen topgallant clewlines 2¼ in., reef tackles 2¼in., buntlines ...... 2 ins.
Mizen royal clewlines 2 in., reef tackle 2¼ in., buntlines .... 21 thds.
Mizen skysail clewlines 2 in., buntlines .... 21 thds.

RUNNING GEAR CORDAGE

Fore and main sheets .... 5 ins.
Fore and main topgallant sheet whips .... 2½ ins.
Mizen and main topgallant sheet whips .... 2¼ ins.
Stay foresail sheet .... 3¼ ins.

Main topmast staysail sheet .... 3½ ins.
Main topgallant staysail sheet .... 3¼ ins.
Main royal staysail sheet .... 2¾ ins.
Mizen topmast staysail sheet .... 3½ ins.
Mizen topgallant staysail sheet .... 2¾ ins.
Mizen royal staysail sheet .... 2¼ ins.
Fore and main staysail sheet .... 3¼ ins.
Mizen staysail sheet .... 2¾ ins.
Fore main skysail sheet .... 2½ ins.
Spanker sheet .... 2¾ ins.
Main staysail sheet .... 3¼ ins.
Fore and main topsail halyards .... 3¼ ins.
Mizen topsail halyards .... 3 ins.
Fore topgallant and main halyards .... 2¾ ins.
Mizen topgallant halyards .... 2¼ ins.
Fore and main royal halyards pandants .... 3½ ins.
Fore and main royal halyards whips .... 2½ ins.
Mizen royal halyards .... 3 ins.
Fore and main skysail halyards .... 2¾ ins.
Main staysail and fore staysail halyards .... 2¾ ins.
Main staysail and stay foresail downhauls .... 2¼ ins.
Jib topsail halyards 2½ in., downhaul .... 24 thds.
Flying jib halyards 2¾ in., whip 2 in., downhaul .... 2 ins.
Outer jib halyards 2¾ in., downhaul .... 2¼ ins.
Inner jib halyards 2¾ in., downhaul .... 2¼ ins.
Fore topmast staysail halyards 3¼ in., whil 2¼ in., downhaul .... 2¼ ins.
Mizen skysail sheet .... 2 ins.
Mizen skysail halyards .... 2¼ ins.

BRACES

Fore and main braces .... 3½ ins.
Crossjack, lower and upper mizen topsail braces .... 3 ins.
Lower and upper, fore and main topsail braces .... 3 ins.
Fore and main topgallant braces .... 2¾ ins.
Mizen topgallant and fore and main royal braces .... 2½ ins.
Mizen royal and fore and main royal braces .... 2¼ ins.
Fore and main skysail braces .... 24 thds.

WIRE LIFTS

Fore main lift .... 3¼ ins.
Crossjack lift .... 2¾ ins.
Lower fore and main topsail lifts .... 3 ins.
Upper fore and main topsail lifts .... 3 ins.
Lower and upper mizen topsail lifts .... 2¾ ins.
Fore and main topgallant lifts .... 2¾ ins.

Mizen topgallant lifts .... 2½ ins.
Fore and main royal lifts .... 2¼ ins.
Fore, main and mizen skysail lifts .... 1¾ ins.

WORKING SAIL INVENTORY

Description		No. of Canvas	No. of Yards in Each	Yards of Lining	No. of Canvas of Linings
Jib topsail	A	5	99	4½	6
Flying jib	B	4	140	8	6
Outer jib	C	3	165	8½	5
Inner jib	C	2	181	8½	4
Fore topmast staysail	E	1	166	6	4
Stay foresail	F	1	120½	5½	4
Jamie Green		6	142	—	—
Foresail	G	1	455	63	4
Lower fore topsail	H	1	203	53	4
Upper fore topsail	I	2	215	41½	4
Fore topgallant sail	J	3	196	36½	5
Fore royal	K	4	102	11	6
Fore skysail	L	6	43	—	—
Square mainsail	R	2	568	72	4
Lower main topsail	S	1	220	55½	4
Upper main topsail	T	2	251	48	4
Main topgallant sail	U	3	225	38½	5
Main royal	V	4	114½	12	6
Main skysail	W	6	51	—	—
Main staysail	M	1	167	6	4
Main topmast staysail	N	3	294	7	5
Main topgallant staysail	O	4	206	5	6
Main royal staysail	P	5	156½	4½	6
Crossjack	Q	4	313	47	6
Lower mizen topsail	Y	1	160	42	4
Upper mizen topsail	X	2	135	30	5
Mizen topgallant sail	AA	4	141	21	6
Mizen royal	BB	5	69	10	6
Mizen skysail	CC	6	34	—	—
Mizen topmast staysail	X	4	168	5	6
Mizen topgallant staysail		5	116	5	6
Mizen royal staysail		6	77	—	—
Spanker	DD	2	242	16	4
Gaff topsail		5	105	10	6
Ring tail		5	163	—	—
Lower studding sail		4	330	—	—
Fore topmast studding sail		4	191	—	—
Fore topgallant studding sail		5	96½	—	—

Description	No. of Canvas	No. of Yards in Each	Yards of Lining	No. of Canvas of Linings
Fore royal studding sail	6	55	—	—
Main topmast studding sail	4	214	—	—
Main topgallant studding sail	5	103	—	—
Main royal studding sail	6	60	—	—
Main skysail studding sail	8	25	—	—

APPENDIX C

CALIPH'S INVENTORY

SAILS

2 flying jibs
2 outer jibs
2 inner jibs
2 fore topmast staysails
1 stay foresail
2 foresails
2 lower fore topsails
2 upper fore topsails
2 topgallant sails
2 royals
2 skysails
2 mainsails
2 lower topsails
2 upper topsails
2 topgallant sails
2 main royals
2 skysails
2 crossjacks
2 mizen lower topsails
2 mizen upper topsails
2 topgallant sails
2 royals
2 skysails
2 spankers
1 gaff topsail
1 ring tail
1 storm main staysail
2 topmast staysails

2 topgallant main staysails
2 royal main staysails
2 mizen topmast staysails
2 mizen topgallant staysails
2 mizen royal staysails
2 mizen Jamie Green
1 jib topsail
2 lower studdingsails
4 topmast studdingsails
4 topgallant studdingsails
3 royal studdingsails
2 skysails
1 capstan cover
2 skylight covers
1 wheel cover
4 boats cover
3 windsails
1 gig awning
3 tarpaulins for each hatch
2 double mast coats for each mast and
    pumps
1 binnacle cover
1 bell cover
1 flag chest
Chain-pipe covers
Awnings for aft with side curtains
Aft awnings galvanized stanchions

SPARE SPARS

1 spare lower yard
1 spare topmast yard
1 spare topsail yard

1 spare jib boom
2 topgallant masts and yards
12 small spars assorted

SHIP CHANDLERY

17 bolts of Edinburgh or Leith canvas
1 patent deep-sea lead, 32 lbs.
1 log keel
6 dozen seaming & 6 doz. roping twine
20 galls. turpentine, in iron cans with brass taps
5 galls. turpentine
2 lbs. black lead
2 lbs. of glue
28 lbs. umber
3 lbs. chrome
1 pot of vermilion
12 lbs. chalk
14 lbs. dryer
1 cwt. oakum
4 palms

½ hide of service leather
2 barrels of Stockholm tar
2 barrels of pitch
1 barrel of bright varnish
½ hide pump leather
4 cwt. black paint
10 cwt. white paint
1 grindstone
12 bath bricks
6 balls cotton
6 rolls wick
1 gross matches
60 gallons olive oil
50 gallons boiled paint-oil in small iron tank with tap
50 gallons raw paint-oil

IRONMONGERY (HARDWARE)

1000 4 d. clasp nails
500 8d. clasp nails
500 10d. clasp nails
500 12d. clasp nails
800 boat nails assorted
200 3 in. batten nails
2 cable stoppers
12 round mouth ballast shovels, No. 3
1000 copper pump tacks
4 oil feeders
1 pitch pot (4 galls.) and ladle
5 lbs. sheet lead
6 brass padlocks for hatches
12 scrapers
4 water drippers
2 japanned safety lamps
1 cook's lamps
2 cabin lamps to cost 40/, not less
2 steerage lamps

2 forecastle lamps
3 funnels, one wood for deck and two copper
1 bread basket
1 sugar canister
2 frying pans
1 tea canister
2 dustpans
12 ivory-handled table knives
1 set scales and weights
2 pair ivory-handled carvers
1 steel
1 candlebox
1 cheese tray
4 corner dishes
1 cream jug
1 tureen
6 egg stands
1 wine funnel

GLASS AND CROCKERY WARE

2 quart decanters cut
2 pint decanters cut
2 dozen tumblers
4 round salts
6 flat meat dishes
4 vegetable dishes
6 sauce tureens, complete
2 butter boats and stands
1 well dish
1 fish drainer
1 salad boat
4 dessert dishes
12 dessert plates
12 egg cups
12 tea cups

2 dozen dinner plates
2 dozen soup plates
2 dozen pudding plates
2 dozen cheese plates
12 coffee mugs
2 round sugar boxes
2 butter tubs
4 slop dishes
4 stone jugs
6 pie dishes
1 brush tray
12 champagne glasses
1 fruit service
1 cream jug

All to be of china service, with ship's name and flag, to be approved of.

CORDAGE

1 coil each, 4½ in. and 4 in. cordage
1 coil each, 3¾ in. and 2¾ in. cordage
1 coil each 3¼ in. and 3½ in. cordage
2 coils each 3 in. cordage
10 coils assorted from 20th ds. down to
　　3 in. additional cordage
½ coil, 4½, 5 and 5¼ in. lanyard rope
2 cwt. of bolts rope, assorted
4 doz. fine 2 yarn and 4 doz. 3 yarn
　　spunyarn
4 doz. amber line, assorted

6 doz. marline
6 doz. houseline
Signal halyards, one for each mast
1 10 in. hawser
1 9 in. hawser, 4 fish lines — 16, 12,
　　8, and 6 oz.
1 7 in. hawser, 26 lbs. of log lines
1 5½ in. hawser, 2 hand leads — one
　　8 lbs. and one 12 lbs.
1 hand lead line 20 fathoms long
1 hand lead line 25 fathoms long

FLAGS

1 ensign
1 code signals
1 code private signals

1 union jack
1 blue peter
1 house flag

MISCELLANEOUS

2 corkscrews
2 coffee mills
1 grater

1 pepper mill
6 skewers
1 cook's saw

1 ladle
1 coffee pot
1 set of measures
1 gravy ladle
2 sauce ladles
1 filler
1 steelyard
1 flour box
1 copper pump
1 hand bell

1 poop bell, engraved
1 axe
2 copper kettles
1 brass guarded lamp
2 screw wrenches
12 pair police handcuffs
1 metal tureen
12 ivory-handled dessert knives
1 waiter
2 dozen wine glasses

ELECTRO-PLATED GOODS

6 dish covers
1 dozen forks
1 dozen forks dessert
1 dozen egg spoons
6 salt spoons
4 mustard spoons
1 pair sugar tongs
2 waiters

2 soup ladles
2 teapots
2 butter knives
12 table spoons
12 tea spoons
12 dessert spoons
1 set of cruets
7 bottles for cruet stand

COOPERAGE

12 deck buckets for quarter deck, brass
   bound
12 galvanized buckets, for main deck,
   brass bound
3 water kegs for crew, 15 galls, each
4 casks, 16 galls, each, with taps
2 casks, 6 galls, each,

4 casks, 120 galls, each, with brass taps
1 wash deck tub
4 bread barges
12 mess kits
1 harness cask
6 spare buckets, galvanized

NAUTICAL INSTRUMENTS

1 brass ball binnacle, complete
1 standard binnacle, complete
1 compass of standing binnacle
1 Robertson's azimuth deviation
   detector, complete
1 storm compass — compound card
1 plain compass
1 cabin compass
1 best English lever clock

1 telescope
1 marine barometer
1 aneroid
1 best speaking trumpet, with ship's
   name
1 patent fog horn
1 patent log
2-28 sea, and 2-14 sea log glasses

GUNS

1 pair 6 lbs. cannonades mounted complete, to have brass locks
10 best percussion muskets and bayonets (Enfield rifle)
10 best pistols
12 round shot balls
2 dozen skyrockets
2 dozen wooden cartridges
10 sea-service swords

1 box patent blue-lights with discharge
100 minnie balls
50 pistol balls
2 lbs. best powder
1 copper magazine fitted with a sufficient quantity of ammunition to be approved of
1 arm chest

SPARE BLOCKS

2 large purchase blocks
8 single 7 in. blocks bushed
4 single 10 in. blocks bushed
4 single 9 in. blocks bushed
6 single 8 in. blocks bushed
6 single 7 in. blocks bushed

12 single bushed blocks for deck leads
1 dozen bushed sheaves from 7 to 10 in.
1 dozen steel pins
1 dozen hickory handspikes

BRUSHES

24 ground paint brushes assorted
1 heath brush
1 long brush
8 paint scrubbers
3 deck scrubbers
2 tar brushes

12 pencil brushes
1 set shoe brushes
6 pencis besoms
9 each paint and dust brushes
6 sash tools

SUNDRIES

Ship's bell, with name, to weigh 60 lbs.
Carpenter's bench and vice.
2 hold ladders (wood,) independent of fixed iron ladder.
3 'tween deck ladders.
Rope ladder for side of ship
Ladder for passengers, of teak, and fitted with brass stanchions
2 doz. belaying pins — spare
Copper pump for tanks
3 spare washers and glasses for lower side lights.
12 capstan bars, 12 chain hooks.
2 main deck stoppers, with hoops and thimbles.
2 fish hooks, 2 hen coops, 1 doz. belaying pins — spare
2 large gins and chains, 1 pigstye, 1 doz, spare eyebolts

Bread tanks for nine month's bread.
2 hard boards for ship's main rail
2 hardwood chaffing boards for fenders.
2 skeads for ship's side.
1 medicine chest, stationary as required.
2 stoppers and shank painters.
Table linen to be supplied to the value of, say, fifteen pounds sterling.

The articles enumerated in the foregoing inventory to be supplied of the best quality, and subject to the approval of the Owner's Inspector; and should anything be omitted in said inventory, the builders to supply the same, free of charge and of the best quality, in order for the proper equipment of the vessel for sea, and equal to any merchant ship built in Great Britain.

1 coffee canister, 14 lbs. ditto, large tea ditto
500 clasp nails, 500 2½ in. nails, 3 canisters, polishing powder, 1 bell — steward's.
1 plate basket, 1 pewter jug.
Stateroom lamps — 1 each for masters 2 mate's ditto
2 bake pans, and 1 iron.
2 spirit taps, 2 pairs lamp scissors, 1 limejuice measure.
1 mincing knife, 2 pairs snuffers and trays plated.
1 crumb brush, 2 cook's knives, cook's stone knife.
Board scouring brush, 1 rolling pin, egg whisk, 1 sieve, 1 cleaver.
4 board tin, 1 duster, 2 pairs candlesticks for cabin — plated.
1 vegetable grater, 1 sugar nipper, 2 plate brushes.
1 pewter bottle for captain's room, 1 brand iron with ship's name.
1 Dullo foghorn, with screwed brass shanks for pings.
1 pepper box, 2 plate leathers, 1 doz. patty pans, 1 shark hook.
6 hand stones, 6 serving mallets, 6 serving boards, 6 sail hooks.
6 doz. sail needles, 6 yards of sheathing felt, 6 cork fenders.
4 life buoys, 2 pairs of claw hooks, 2 crowbars, 24 connecting links.
4 cold chisels, 1 doz. clip hooks, 24 fish hooks, 12 single ditto assorted.
4 doz. firelocks, 1 pair graims, 1 harpoon, 1 handsaw.
4 galvanized tanks, lamp oil 45 gals., and paint oil 40 gals., each to have brass taps
    and holes at top of each for cleaning them out, with screw at covers.
1 grapnel, 30 lbs. weight.
6 tanks for paint, 1 pair of rigging screws.
2 chain puncheon slings, 6 deck lights, 18 marlinespikes.
2 pair crate hooks, brass signal lamps.
1 callipers.

APPENDIX D

CALIPH CARGO MANIFEST
OCTOBER 12, 1869

(Typical of general cargo carried by clippers
on the outward passage to China and Australia.)

26 cks 5 b beer in glass 45	10 cs 8650 y dyed cotton 395
15 cs 3¼ b beer in glass 15	2 cs 400 lbs paper 31
60 cs 12¾ b beer in glass 120	account books 3
57 cs 12½ b beer in glass 49	stationery 2
25 cs 5½ b beer in glass 20	50 tons lead 1000
7 cs 1¼ b beer in glass 12	50 bls 120000 y pln cottons 2085
15 cs 3¼ b beer in glass 15	2400 bdls 60 t nail nod 420
62 hhds 3720 gls Fr wine	1 cs effects 100
1 cs 1 c glass manufctr	3 cs 11 c. hardware ....
20 cs 43 c wax candles	30 bls 58500 y
1 cs 7 c iron manufctr	pln cottons 790
10 cs 20 c paper	20 bls 48000 y
40 cs goods manufctr 100	pln cottons 850
2 cs 4 c books	12 bls 2400 lbs hay 7
1 cs 1 harmonium	6 cks 9 c oats 5
75 cs 150 gls brandy	5 bls 12000 y pln cottons 210
100 cs 172 gls brandy	12 cs 5586 y woollens 800
30 cs 52 gls brandy	3 cs 2800 y pln cottons 110
1 cs 3 c iron manufcts	1 cs provisions 10
25 cs 500 lbs wax vestas	250 bxs 12½ tinplates 285
50 cs 90 gls brandy	1 cs 6 gls spirits wine ....
54 cs 308 gls spirits wine	3 cs 5 gls brandy ....
1 cs 6 gls spirits wine	30 cs 60 gls Fr w wine ....
12 bls 26000 y pln ctns 600	1 cs 4 gls mixed spirits ....
14 pkgs stationery 150	3 lbs chloroform ....
50 tons pig iron 150	40 cs woollen manufactures 3170
100 bxs 5 t tin plates 120	2 cs apparel 30
4 cks 22 c green copperas 6	10 cs cotton manufactures 330

2 cs tools	37
1 cs leather manufactures	60
10 cs 60 gls wine	
1 cs 8 gls purified spirits	
3 cs 25 gls spirits	
12 cs 15 lbs flint glass	100
188 bls 358500 y pln ctns	4210
20 cs 23000 y dyed ctns	720
10 cs 6000 y worsted stuffs	450
5 cs 3000 y worsted stuffs	225
10 cs 6000 y worsted stuffs	450
10 cs 1560 y worsted stuffs	410
50 bls 95700 y pln cottons	1270
40 bls 8 kgs 77500 y pln cottons	1240
5 cs 3000 y worsted stuffs	225
4 cs 6000 y worsted & cottons	260
1 ck 6 gls r wine	
20 cs 28000 y ptd cottons	430
1 cs haberdashery	5
1 ble 2263 y worsted stuffs	150
100 bls 120000 y pln cottons	2142
50 trusses 24000 y worsted	1654
25 trusses 1230 y worsted	827
1 cs 3 gls cherry brandy	
25 cks plain cottons	168
40 dms 200 gls turpentine	22
22 brls 773 gls linseed oil	114
2 casks lanterns	22
1 crate ironmongery	8
2 rolls 4½ c lead	5
20 cs haberdashery	400
3 crates earthenware	14
10 cs 14000 y print cottons	490
30 drms 5 brls 325 gls linseed oil	42
5 drms 25 gls turpentine	3
1 cs 8 gls varnish	6
10 cks painter's colours	97
2 cs saddlery	50
1 cs stationery	24
1 cs brushes	3
9 cs furniture	24
75 trus 36000 y worsted stuffs	2480
20 bls 39000 y pln cottons	600

6 cs 6480 y cotton velvet	258
5 cs 2400 y worsteds	375
6 cs 9000 y cotton & worsted	330
50 bls 24000 y woolens	1450
110 cs 288000 y prnt cottons	4099
3 cs apothecary wares	12
6 bls 2500 y canvas	200
2 cs 8 prs blankets	20
52 lead lines	30
5 cs disinfecting fluid	3
10 cs 12000 y cotton & worsted crapes	520
6 cks apothecary wares	60
1 cs books	10
1 cs 193 lb paper	15
2 cks potas water	5
1 cs portmanteaus	12
2 hhds chinaware	40
1 cs account books	18
1 cs 430 lb paper	40
1 cs envelopes	6
1 cs 80 lb. packing paper	2
2 cs 130 y floor cloth	25
10 cks lemonade in glass	21
1 cs electro plate	22
1 ck earthenware	14
2 cs drugs	6
1 kg 36 lbs copper nails	2
240 bxs 12½ t tin plates	285
15 cs 9000 y worsteds	775
10 cs 12750 y fustians	500
60 bls 71760 y pln cottons	1630
1000 bxs 1000 c window glass	
2 bls 700 lbs. corks	
1 cs billiard chalk	3
45 cs 4250 y worsted	1575
10 cs 54060 y cld cottons	1165
56 bls 99400 y pln cottons	1212
10 cs 6000 worsteds	450
4 cs 6000 y wln and cottons	260
161 bls 193950 y pln cottons	3425
25 cs umbrellas	450
10 cs 8300 y dyed cottons	320
5 cs 1400 y worsted stuffs	300
101 bls 128250 y pln cottons	2433
1 cs haberdashery	25

113 bls 20 cs 5649000 y
    pln ctns 3757
17 cs 29560 y pntd cottons 391
121 bls 145200 y pln cottons ... 2904
1 ck apothecary wares 5
13 cs oilman's stores 58
1 cs canvas hose 80
33 pkgs 5 t rope 300
10 cs 6000 y worsted 450
8 bls 360 pair blankets 360
25 cs 22286 y cotton velvets ... 1295
35 bls 20 cs 89500 y
    pln cotns 1403
1 cs 10 doz straw hats 16
5 doz woollen hats 10
10 cs 1400 y prnted cottons 235
50 bls 93750 y pln cottons 1400
8 cs 1920 y worsteds 300
22 cs 3300 y worsted & cotton . 880
185 bls 252100 y pln cotton 3811
5 cs 720 y woollens 200
150 bls 180000 y pln cottons ... 3525
1 trunk books 4
10 cs 6000 y worsteds 476
20 cs 12000 y worsteds 900
1 cs 600 y worsteds 45
3 bls 1900 y flannel 120
1 cs 400 y woollens 80
1 cs haberdashery 25
4 cs 6000 y wln and cotton 260
1 cs preserves 2

11 bls 20000 y pln cottons 297
39 cs 46050 y dyed cottons 1100
50 bls 2 cs 96200 y pln cotns .. 1220
10 bls 4645 y woollens 698
50 bls 96250 y pln cottons 1250
5 cs 2421 y worsteds 345
4 cs biscuits 150
21 cs 42000 y pln cottons 735
9 cs 218 bls 291000
    y pln cotns 1220
10 bls 4645 y woollens 698
50 bls 96250 y pln cottons 1250
5 cs 2421 y worsteds 345
4 cs biscuits 150
21 cs 42000 y pln cottn 5645
9 cs 218 bls 291000
    y pln cottn 5645
8 cs 12000 y worsteds
    & cottns 520
22 cs 24 doz felt hats 91
80 bls 48000 y pln cotton 1020
5 cs 5259 y dyed cottons 260
25 bls 12000 y woolens 755
60 bls 99200 y pln cottons 2000
17 bls 27560 y prnt cottons 374
1 cs 900 y woollens 90
8 cs 800 y canvas 180
1 cs sardines 24
20 bls 24000 y pln cottons 450
40 bls 77011 pln cottons 920

APPENDIX E

SOME FAMOUS BRITISH TEA CLIPPERS

Ship	Tonnage	Length	Breadth	Depth	Builder	Date Built
Stornoway	506	157-8	28-8	17-8	Hall, Aberdeen	1850
Chrysolite	471	149-3	26-1	17-0	Hall, Aberdeen	1851
Lord of the Isles	770	190-9	27-8	18-5	Scott, Greenock	1853
Falcon	937	191-4	32-2	20-0	Steele, Greenock	1859
Fiery Cross	888	185-0	31-7	19-2	Chaloner, Liverpool	1860
Flying Spur	735	184-0	31-4	19-4	Hall, Aberdeen	1860
Min	629	174-5	29-8	19-3	Steele, Greenock	1861
White Adder	915	191-4	34-0	20-7	Bilbe, London	1862
Taeping	767	183-7	31-1	19-9	Steele, Greenock	1863
Serica	708	185-9	31-1	19-6	Steele, Greenock	1863
Belted Will	812	186-4	32-4	20-8	Feel-Workington	1863
Ariel	852	197-4	33-9	21-0	Steele, Greenock	1865
Sir Lancelot	886	197-6	33-7	21-0	Steele, Greenock	1865
Taitsing	815	192-0	31-5	20-1	Connell	1865
Titania	879	200-0	36-0	21-0	Steele, Greenock	1866
Spindrift	899	219-4	35-6	20-2	Connell	1867
Lahloo	799	191-6	32-9	19-9	Steele, Greenock	1867
Leander	883	210-0	35-2	20-8	Lawrie, Glasgow	1867
Undine	796	182-6	35-1	19-5	Pile	1867
Forward-Ho	943	193-7	33-6	20-6	Stephen	1867
Thermopylae	948	212-0	36-0	20-9	Hood, Aberdeen	1868
Windhover	847	201-1	34-0	20-3	Steele, Greenock	1868
Kaisow	795	193-2	32-0	20-3	Steele, Greenock	1868
Cutty Sark	921	212-5	36-0	21-0	Scott & Linton	1869
Wylo	799	189-9	32-1	20-2	Steele, Greenock	1869
Norman Court	834	197-4	33-0	20-0	Inglis	1869
Caliph	914	215-1	36-1	20-4	Hall, Aberdeen	1869
BlackAdder	918	216-6	35-2	20-5	Maudsley, London	1870
Hallowe'en	920	216-6	35-2	20-5	Maudsley, London	1870
Lothair	794	191-8	33-5	19-0	Walker	1870

APPENDIX F

TEA PASSAGE RECORDS OF SOME TEA CLIPPERS 1870 TO 1879

	1870	1871	1872	1873	1874	1875	1876	1877	1878	1879
Ariel	—	114	*	—	—	—	—	—	—	—
Cutty Sark	110	108	121	117	119	123	109	123	—	—
Falcon	108	—	109**	—	—	—	—	—	—	—
Fiery Cross	117	—	—	—	—	—	—	—	—	—
Forward Ho	119	118	—	131	131	110	—	109	—	—
Hallow'en	—	—	—	90	91	92	102	97	—	135
Lahloo	98	116	*	—	—	—	—	—	—	—
Leander	98	—	—	—	—	—	—	—	—	128
Norman Court	105	111	96	116	113	120	107	—	—	117
Serica	118	—	—	—	—	—	—	—	—	—
Sir Lancelot	104	—	122	127	124	—	—	—	—	128
Taeping	112	—	*	—	—	—	—	—	—	—
Taitsing	121	—	114	—	—	—	—	—	—	—
Thermopylae	105	106	115	101	104	115	115	102	110	—
Thyatira	118	108	123	106	—	—	—	—	—	—
Titania	112	93	116	138	100	—	—	—	100	—
Undine	105	111	115	133	113	116	111	—	—	145
Windhover	99	—	—	—	—	—	128	125	121	—
Wylo	112	—	—	127	—	—	—	111	115	

*Wrecked

**Clark: *The Clipper Ship Era* claims Falcon was wrecked off the coast of Java in 1871. Lubbock's *Log of the Cutty Sark* lists Falcon in the 1872 homeward passage.

APPENDIX G

DETAILS OF CUTTY SARK'S
CHINA TEA CARGO

Freight Rate	Date Departed	Cargo Weight	From Port	Arrived English Channel	Date	Days Out
L310s	June 25, 1870	1,305,821	Shanghai	BeachyHead	Oct 12	110
L3	Sept. 4, 1871	1,315,100	Shanghai	North Foreland	Dec 20	108
L310s	June 18, 1872	1,303,000	Shanghai	Portland	Oct 18	121
L4	July 9, 1873	1,353,072	Shanghai	Deal	Nov 3	117
L5-L4	June 24, 1874	1,270,651	Woosung Pilot	Deal	Oct 20	119
L4	June 21, 1875	1,347,699	Woosung Pilot	Deal	Oct 21	123
L45s	June 9, 1876	1,375,364	Woosung Pilot	Start	Sept 25	109
L45s	June 6, 1877	1,334,000	Woosung Pilot	Scilly	Oct 6	123

APPENDIX H

THE CUTTY SARK'S RECORD AS A WOOL CLIPPER

Departed	Year	From	To	# Bales	Days out	Captain
Dec.	1883	Newcastle N.S.W.	Deal	4289	82	E. Moore
Dec.	1884	Newcastle N.S.W.	Dock	4300	80	E. Moore
Oct.	1885	Sydney	Downs	4465	73	R. Woodget
March	1887	Sydney	Lizard	4296	70	R. Woodget
Dec.	1887	Newcastle N.S.W.	Lizard	4515	69	R. Woodget
Oct.	1888	Sydney	London	4496	86	R. Woodget
Nov.	1889	Sydney	London	4577	75	R. Woodget
Dec.	1890	Sydney	London	4617	93	R. Woodget
Nov.	1891	Sydney	Lizard	4636	83	R. Woodget
Jan.	1893	Sydney	Antwerp	4723	98	R. Woodget
Dec.	1893	Sydney	Hull	5010	93	R. Woodget
Dec.	1894	Brisbane	London	5304	84	R. Woodget

Average weight per bale 400 lbs.
Average value of cargo L100,000 (on basis of 5000 bales)
Freight rate: ½ penny/lb. for washed wool
⅜ penny/lb. for greasy wool

APPENDIX I

MODERN BEAUFORT SCALE
of Winds and the Fully Developed Seas that Result

by F. G. Walton Smith

Beaufort Number	Knots	Nautical Term	Form and Height of Waves in ft.	Code	Effects Observed at Sea	Effects Observed on Land
	Wind			**International**		**Wind Effects**
0	Under 1	Calm			Sea like mirror	Calm; smoke rises vertically
1	1-3	Light air	calm glassy 0	0	Ripples with appearance of scales; no foam crests.	Smoke drift indicates wind direction; vanes do not move.
2	4-6	light breeze	rippled 0-1	1	Small wavelets; crests of glassy appearance, not breaking.	Wind felt on face; leaves rustle; vanes begin to move
3	7-10	gentle breeze	smooth 1-2	2	Large wavelets; crests begin to break; scattered whitecaps.	Leaves, small twigs in constant motion, light flags extended.
4	11-16	moderate breeze	slight 2-4	3	Small waves, becoming longer; numerous whitecaps.	Dust, leaves and loose paper raised up; small branches move.
5	17-21	fresh breeze	moderate 4-8	4	Moderate waves, taking longer form many whitecaps; some spray	Small trees in leaf begin to sway.
6	22-27	strong breeze	rough 8-13	5	Larger waves forming; whitecaps everywhere; more spray	Larger branches of trees in motion; whistling heard in wires.
7	28-33	moderate gale	very rough 13-20	6	Sea heaps up; white foam from breaking waves begins to be blown in streaks.	Whole trees in motion; resistance felt in walking against wind.
8	34-40	fresh gale	very rough 13-20	6	Moderately high waves of greater length; edges of crests begin to break into spindrift; foam is blown in well-marked streaks.	Twigs and small branches broken off trees; progress generally impeded.
9	41-47	strong gale	very rough 13-20	6	High waves; sea begins to roll; dense streaks of foam; spray may reduce visibility.	Slight structural damage occurs; slate blown from roofs.

Taken from the book, *The Seas in Motion*, by F. G. Walton Smith.

10	48-55	whole gale	High 20-30	7	Very high waves with overhanging crests; sea takes white appearance as foam is blown in very dense streaks; rolling is heavy and visibility reduced.	Seldom experienced on land trees broken or uprooted; considerable structural damage occurs.
11	56-63	storm	very high 30-45	8	Exceptionally high waves; sea covered with white foam patches; visibility still more reduced.	Very rarely experienced on land; usually accompanied by widespread damage.
12	64-71	Hurricane	Phenomenal over 45	9	Air filled with foam; sea completely white with driving spray; visibility greatly reduced.	Very rarely experienced on land; usually accompanied by widespread damage.
13	72-80					
14	81-89					
15	90-99					
16	100-108					
17	109-118					

APPENDIX J

Condition of the Sea Caused by the Wind &
Sails Commonly Set Accordingly

Beaufort Number	Knots	Nautical Term	Form and Height of Waves in ft.	Effects Observed at Sea	Sails Set
0	Under 1	Calm		Sea like mirror	
1	1-3	Light air	calm glassy 0	Ripples with appearance of scales; no foam crests	Courses, Topsails, T'Gallant Sails
2	4-6	Light breeze	rippled 0-1	Small wavelets; crests	
3	7-10	gentle breeze; T'gallant breeze	smooth 1-2	Large wavelets; crests begin to break; scattered whitecaps.	Royals, Spanker, Jib Flying jib and all light sails.
4	11-16	moderate breeze; fresh T'gallant breeze	slight 2-4	Small waves, becoming longer; numerous whitecaps.	
5	17-21	fresh breeze; whole topsail breeze	moderate 4-8	Moderate waves, taking longer form many whitecaps; some spray.	Full & by, Royals. In a sea way to Royals & Flying jib taken in; to two reefs in the topsails.
6	22-27	strong breeze	rough 8-13	Larger waves forming; whitecaps everywhere; more spray.	Full & by single reef & T'gallants. Much sea two reefs in the topsails to taking in T'gallants.
7	28-33	moderate gale; reefed topsail	very rough 13-20	Sea heaps up; white foam from breaking waves begins to be blown in streaks.	Full & by, double reef & jib; to treble reefed topsails, reefed spanker & jib
8	34-40	fresh gale; scudding sails	very rough 13-20	moderately high waves of greater length; edges of crests begin to break into spindrift; foam is blown in well-marked streaks	full & by, triple reef to close reefed topsails, reefed courses, to taking in spanker, jib, fore & mizzen topsails.
9	41-47	strong gale; half storm		High waves; sea begins to roll; dense streaks of foam spray may reduce visibility	close reefed fore & main reefed foresail and fore staysail, close hauled, to reefed courses, close reefed main topsail fore staysail, mizzen trysail to taking in main sail.

10	48-55	whole gale; whole storm	high 20-30	very high waves with overhanging crests; sea takes white appearance as foam is blown in very dense streaks; rolling is heavy and visibility reduced	close reefed main topsail and reefed foresail and fore staysail, to close reefed main topsail, storm staysails or close-reefed main topsail only.
11	56-63	Storm	very high 30-45	Exceptionally high waves sea covered with white foam patches; visibility still more reduced.	storm staysails to bare poles.
12	64-71			Air filled with foam; sea completely white with driving spray; visibility greatly reduced.	Bare poles
13	72-80	Hurricane	phenomenal over 45		
14	81-89				
15	90-99				
16	100-108				
17	109-118				

BIBLIOGRAPHY

Abbey, Charles A. .... *Before the Mast in the Clippers* 1937
Biddlecomb, Capt. George .. *The Art of Rigging* 1848
Bray, Mary M. .... *A Sea Trip in Clipper Ship Days* 1920
British Admiralty .... *Chart; Carimata Strait* 1852
British Admiralty. .... *Chart; Mindoro Strait to Hong Kong* 1859
British Admiralty .... *The China Sea Directory* .... Vol. 1 1867
    Hydrographic Office   Vol. 2 1868
Bushell, Charles .... *The Riggers Guide* 1893
Cable, Boyd .... *A Hundred Year History of the
                             Peninsular and Oriental Steam
                             Navigation Co.* 1937
Carr, Frank C. C. .... *The Cutty Sark* 1966
Carr, Frank C. C. .... *The Restoration of the Cutty Sark* 1965
Chapelle, Howard I. .... *The Baltimore Clipper* 1930
                             The History of American Sailing Ships 1935
                             The Search for Speed Under Sail 1967
Chapman, Charles .... *All About Ships* 1869
Charles-Roux, J. .... *L'Isthme et le canal de Suez (2 vols.)* 1901
Chatterton, E. Kible .... *The Old East Indiamen* 1933
Chichester, Sir Francis ..... *Along the Clipper Way* 1966
Clark, Arthur H. .... *The Clipper Ship Era* 1920
Clark, Francis G. .... *The Seaman's Manual* 1836
Conrad, Joseph .... *The Secret Sharer* 1924
Cowans, David .... *Anecdotes of a Life on the Ocean* 1871
Cutler, C. C. .... *Five Hundred Sailing Records of
                             American Built Ships* 1952
Cutler, C. C. .... *Greyhounds of the Sea* 1930
Davis, Charles C. .... *Ships of the Past* 1929
Ellis, Capt. F. W. .... *Round Cape Horn in Sail* 1890
Fairburn, William .... *Treatise on Iron Shipbuilding* 1865
Fincham, John .... *History of Naval Architecture* 1851
Fox-Smith, C. .... *The Return of the Cutty Sark* 1925
Harlow, Frederick P. .... *The Making of a Sailor* 1928
Horsburgh, James .... *Chart; China; Eastern Passage* 1848

Howe & Matthews .... *American Clipper Ships (2 vols.)* 1926
King, E. R. .... *Ship Handling* 1954
Knight, Austin M. .... *Modern Seamanship* 1903
La Grange, Helen .... *Clipper Ships* 1936
Laing, Alexander .... *Clipper Ship Men* 1944
Longridge, C. Nepean .... *The Cutty Sark (2 vols.)* 1933
Low, Charles P. .... *Some Recollections by Capt. Charles P. Low
                              in the China Trade* 1906
Low, William Gillman ...... *A. A. Low & Bros. Fleet of Clipper Ships* ... 1919
Lubbock, Basil .... *The China Clippers* 1914
                            The Colonial Clippers 1921
                            The Log of the Cutty Sark 1924
                            Round the Horn Before the Mast 1902
                            Sail (3 vols.) 1938
MacGregor, David R. .... *The Tea Clippers* 1952
McKay, Richard .... *Some Famous Sailing Ships and Their Builder,
                             Donald McKay* 1928
Masefield, John .... *Salt Water Poems* 1916
Rogers, Lt. John .... *Chart; China Sea Northeast
                             Chart; Gaspar Strait* 1854
Rosser, William H. .... *Indian Ocean Directory* 1866
Scott, J. L. .... *A Survey of the Cutty Sark in 1937* 1941
Sherwan, Andrew .... *The Great Days of Sail* 1927
Smith, F. G. Walton .... *The Seas in Motion* 1972
Smith, H. .... *Pilot Guide, Strait of Gaspar* 1852
Sperry, A. .... *All Sails Set* 1935
Staveacre, F. W. F. .... *Tea and Tea Dealing* 1929
Tryckare, Tre. .... *The Lore of Ships* 1963
Ukers, William H. .... *All About Tea* 1935
Villiers, Allen .... *The Way of a Ship* 1953
Wilson, A. T. .... *The Suez Canal, It's Past, Present
                             and Future* 1933
Wilson, Charles .... *Chart; South China Sea* 1867

INDEX

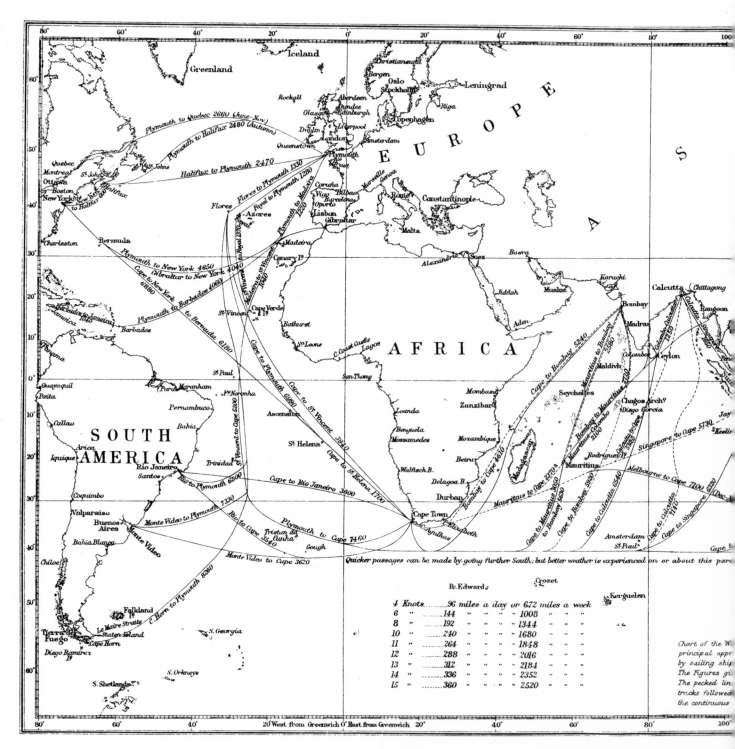

THE PRINCIPAL TRADE R

Based on Admiralty Chart 1078, by pe